Priests, Prophets AND Sages

CATHOLIC PERSPECTIVES ON THE OLD TESTAMENT

LESLIE J. HOPPE, O.F.M.

ST. ANTHONY MESSENGER PRESS

Cincinnati, Ohio

RESCRIPT

In accord with the *Code of Canon Law,* I hereby grant my permission to publish *Priests, Prophets and Sages: Catholic Perspectives on the Old Testament* by Leslie J. Hoppe, O.F.M.

Most Reverend Carl K. Moeddel
Vicar General and Auxiliary Bishop of the Archdiocese of Cincinnati
Cincinnati, Ohio
January 3, 2006

The permission to publish is a declaration that a book or pamphlet is considered to be free from doctrinal or moral error. It is not implied that those who have granted the permission to publish agree with the contents, opinions or statements expressed.

Scripture passages have been taken from *New Revised Standard Version Bible,* copyright ©1989 by the Division of Christian Education of the National Council of the Churches of Christ in the U.S.A., and used by permission. All rights reserved.

Cover and book design by Mark Sullivan
Cover painting: *Moses Destroying the Tablets of the Law* (1659), Rembrandt van Rijn
Cover photo: Bildarchiv Preussischer Kulturbesitz/Art Resource, NY

LIBRARY OF CONGRESS CATALOGING-IN-PUBLICATION DATA

Hoppe, Leslie J.
Priests, prophets, and sages : Catholic perspectives on the Old Testament / Leslie J. Hoppe.
p. cm.
ISBN 0-86716-697-5 (pbk. : alk. paper)
1. Bible. O.T.—Introductions. 2. Catholic Church—Doctrines.
I. Title.
BS1140.3.H67 2006
221.6'1—dc22
2006000175

ISBN-13: 978-0-86716-697-2
ISBN-10: 0-86716-697-5

Copyright ©2006 Leslie J. Hoppe, O.F.M. All rights reserved.

Published by St. Anthony Messenger Press.
28 W. Liberty St.
Cincinnati, OH 45202
www.AmericanCatholic.org

Printed in the United States of America.

Printed on acid-free paper.

06 07 08 09 10 5 4 3 2 1

CONTENTS

INTRODUCTION

I t has been more than forty years since Vatican II issued *Dei Verbum*, its document on divine revelation. This document did more to engage Catholics in the reading and study of the Bible than any other previous church pronouncement. Almost overnight parish Bible study groups began forming. The curricula on all levels of Catholic education—from grammar schools to seminaries—were reworked to include more Scripture study. Catholic publishers began issuing more books on topics related to the Bible. Catholic magazines like *The Bible Today*, devoted to popular appreciation of the Scriptures, made their appearance. The Bible became more central not only to the renewed liturgy of the church, but it also became a focus of the devotional life of Catholics. "Bible vigils" came into vogue. Catholics read the Bible daily as part of their spiritual disciplines. They began praying with the Bible. The Bible literally exploded onto the Catholic scene in the years immediately following Vatican II.

Despite all these positive developments, there were challenges to overcome before the Scriptures could take their rightful place in Catholic life. After the first flush of enthusiasm in the immediate post-conciliar period, people began to recognize that reading and appreciating the Scriptures does indeed require spiritual and intellectual discipline. The Bible comes from another time and from other cultures. Bridging these temporal and cultural gaps is not a simple matter. In the face of this challenge, a small minority of Catholics has embraced a fundamentalist-like approach to the Scriptures: "The Bible means what it says and says what it means." Most Catholics, however, recognize that the meaning of biblical texts is not immediately self-evident. They read the Scriptures with the help of study Bibles such as *The Catholic Study Bible* or *The New Oxford Annotated Bible*. They work through commentaries. They keep current with the state of biblical studies by reading periodical literature. Some attend parish or diocesan-sponsored programs of biblical studies.

This book aims to contribute to maintaining the enthusiasm for the Scriptures among Catholics. Many have found reading the Old Testament very challenging. Its religious perspectives appear to differ from those of the more familiar New Testament. There are questions about its historical value. Was Jonah really swallowed by a great fish? Then there are the violence and wars that seem to be central to the Old Testament but alien to the nonviolence advocated by Jesus. Most troubling of all, the God of the Old Testament does not appear to be the God about whom Jesus preached. This book tries to deal with some of these issues and respond to some of those questions. It tries to show that the Old Testament is not as alien to modern religious thought as it might first appear—that the Old Testament can make a valuable contribution to believers as they shape their lives of conversion in response to Jesus' proclamation of the Good News.

An important part of the church's treasure is its inheritance from ancient Israel and early Judaism: the Old Testament. The books that make up the Old Testament reflect the encounter between God and our ancestors in faith—in all its dimensions and mystery. Catholics ought to read, study and pray with these books because their lives too are bound up with the very God who spoke through ancient Israel's priests, prophets and sages—the God who spoke finally and definitively through Jesus Christ. In coming to grips with their life with God today, believers ought to be "like the master of a household who brings out of his treasure what is new and what is old" (Matthew 13:52).

A very basic question is posed at the beginning of this book: What should we call the collection of books commonly known as the "Old Testament"? A recent Vatican pronouncement referred to this collection as "the Jewish Scriptures." Other Christians have suggested different names. The second chapter deals with what books are included in the Old Testament. Many Catholics realize that not all Christians agree on what books make up the Old Testament. What is the reason for these disagreements? The third chapter deals with a central concern for Christians who read the Old Testament: ancient Israel's concept of God. The notion of

Israel as a "chosen people"—an exceptionally difficult and personal problem for Paul—is the subject of the fourth chapter. The various ways the people of ancient Israel experienced the Word of God is the topic of the fifth chapter. The sixth chapter deals with an issue that those who read the Old Testament have to face from the very first pages of Genesis: the Old Testament as a historical text. The final chapter focuses on how readers today can find meaning in the biblical text, which was produced so long ago.

Each chapter concludes with a few "Questions for Reflection," which can help begin the processing of the material in the chapter. Also, groups gathered for Bible study may find these questions a way to begin a discussion of some of the issues raised in the chapter. Following these questions is a short bibliography ("For Further Reading") that provides readers interested in probing the chapter's topic more deeply with some books that they can consult.

It is not possible to deal with every challenge that emerges as Catholics today read the Old Testament. But this book shows that these challenges are not insurmountable. No believer ought to put aside the Old Testament because its books raise questions for the contemporary reader. Any book worth reading ought to engage the reader. The Old Testament does just that. It supports believers, challenges them, encourages them and, above all, calls them to greater commitment and more complete obedience.

One day someone asked Jesus to summarize the value of the Scriptures for believers of his day. Jesus quoted two texts from the Old Testament in formulating his answer—an answer that clarifies for today's Christians what the Old Testament is about:

> [Jesus said] "'You shall love the Lord your God with all your heart, and with all your soul, and with all your mind.' This is the greatest and first commandment. And a second is like it: 'You shall love your neighbor as yourself.' On these two commandments hang all the law and prophets." (Matthew 22:37–40; see also Mark 12:29–31; Luke 10:27; see Deuteronomy 6:5; Leviticus 19:18)

CHAPTER ONE

What Do We Call These Books?

C hristianity is the only religion that accepts texts from another religious tradition as normative for its faith and life. The texts that form the first part of the Christian Bible, the books from Genesis to Malachi, were produced by those who believed in Yahweh, a patron deity of the two ancient Israelite kingdoms and the God of the Jews. The books that were composed by those who believed in Jesus as the Christ form the second part of the Christian Bible and are known collectively as the New Testament.

The word "testament" is derived from the Latin word *testamentum,* which is the word used by Jerome to translate the Hebrew and Greek words for "covenant" when he produced a Latin translation of the Bible in the fourth century A.D. The concept of the covenant is central to both parts of the Bible. Luke 22:20 has Jesus say that the cup of wine that he will pass among his disciples is "the new covenant in my blood." Paul uses the same language in 1 Corinthians 11:25, claiming that he received these words from the Risen Lord himself (see verse 23). Also, Christians from the earliest time considered themselves the heirs of the promise of a "new covenant" that the prophet Jeremiah proclaimed (31:31–34). So it is no surprise that the Christians called their sacred texts "the New Covenant" or "the New Testament." And if the Christian Scriptures are "the New Testament," then the holy books the church has accepted from ancient Israel and early Judaism are "the Old Testament" or the "Old Covenant," a term that Paul used to speak of these books—or at least of the Books of Moses (see 2 Corinthians 3:14).

The church, in its official documents on the Bible, generally uses this nomenclature (Old Testament—New Testament) in speaking of the two parts of the Christian Bible. But the Pontifical Biblical Commission's 2001 document entitled *The Jewish People and Their Sacred Scriptures in the Christian Bible* also uses another term for the Old Testament: "the Jewish Scriptures." This change in nomenclature reflects a growing concern for improving Jewish-Christian relationships—a concern of the Second Vatican Council evident in the section devoted to Judaism in its Declaration on Non-Christian Religions, *Nostra Aetate*. While the name "Old Testament" is a Christian name for Jewish Scriptures, the Jews use several names for the collection of their sacred texts. One is *Tanakh,* which is a Hebrew acronym for the three divisions of the Hebrew Scriptures (*Torah* [the Pentateuch], *Nevi'im* [the Prophets] and *Kethuvim* [the Writings]). Another is *Miqra,* which is derived from the Hebrew verb meaning "to call/read." This word signifies that the books in the collection are those read during synagogue worship. A third

Hebrew name is *sifre haqqodesh* (Holy Books), although this phrase is not always used for the Scriptures alone but sometimes refers to other Jewish religious literature. The expression "Old Testament" reflects an appropriation of these Jewish sacred books by the church, but the term "Jewish Scriptures" sets these books firmly within their own religious context. Additionally, the adjective "old" might be understood as "out-of-date," "irrelevant" or "antiquated." Again, this represents a pejorative Christian evaluation of the books sacred to Judaism. Some Christians believe that the church ought to abandon the term "Old Testament" in favor of an expression like the "Jewish Scriptures."

There have been several other attempts at replacing "Old Testament" with another name for the books that form the first part of the Christian Bible. One of these is "the Hebrew Bible," which is similar to the term used by the Pontifical Biblical Commission. *The Oxford Annotated Bible* (NRSV) has chosen to use "Hebrew Bible" rather than Old Testament. Catholics, however, will have a problem with this phrase, because the collection of books from ancient Israel and early Judaism that the Catholic church regards as inspired and normative for its faith and life includes books that are not in the Hebrew Bible: Tobit, Judith, Wisdom, Ecclesiasticus (Sirach), Baruch, 1 and 2 Maccabees plus additions to the books of Daniel and Esther. Catholics refer to these books as "the deuterocanonical books" while Protestants call them "the Apocrypha." The former term implies that their character as inspired texts arises from their inclusion in a second collection of Jewish religious texts: the Septuagint (an early Greek translation of the Hebrew Bible and other religious texts). *Apocrypha* is the Greek word for "hidden" and is used to refer to books on the fringes of the authoritative collection of the two Testaments.

The Bible used by Orthodox Christians contains several more Jewish religious texts not found in the Hebrew Bible. Protestant Christians include only the books of the Hebrew Bible in their collection of sacred texts. The wider collection of books in the Roman Catholic and Orthodox traditions reflects the usage of the early church. The Septuagint became the Bible of the early church since the church was primarily a Greek-speaking, rather than a Hebrew-speaking, community. In fact by Jesus' day most Jews no longer used Hebrew for everyday speech but favored Aramaic instead. Hebrew was a liturgical language for the Jews, much like Latin was for Catholics before Vatican II. Some scholars suggest that Jesus and his disciples were bilingual—conversant in both Aramaic and Greek—since they came from Galilee, a region where contact with the Greek-speaking population of Roman Palestine would have been common.

Another phrase that is sometimes used in place of "Old Testament" is "First Testament" or "Prime Testament." The value of these expressions is that they avoid the negative connotations of "old." The problem is that for Christians the New Testament is their "prime" or "first" testament. While this is not true chronologically speaking, it is nonetheless true from a theological perspective. Christians read the Old Testament because of the revelation of Jesus Christ in the New Testament. It is accurate to say that the Bible for the first Christians was the Old Testament. Still, once the

Scriptures testifying to Christ were produced, they had primacy in shaping Christian faith and life.

What is the proper way to speak of the first part of the Christian Bible—the books from Genesis to Malachi? One writer suggests "Shared Testament," which is fine from the Christian perspective but may not be a solution entirely welcome by all Jews. The *New American Bible,* produced under the auspices of the United States Conference of Catholic Bishops, continues the use of the term "Old Testament." Each of the alternatives to this phrase has some drawbacks. "Old Testament" at least has a history of usage behind it. But to use it authentically, Christians will have to ignore the sectarian and pejorative connotations of "Old."

While recognizing the problems in finding a perfect term for the books of Genesis to Malachi in the Christian Bible, this book will use the term "Old Testament." This term establishes chronology as well as emphasizing the connection to the New Testament. As Jesus said to his disciples when he instructed them in the mysteries of the kingdom of heaven:

> ...every scribe who has been trained for the kingdom of
> heaven is like the master of a household who brings out of
> his treasure what is new and what is old. (Matthew 13:52)

QUESTIONS FOR REFLECTION

1. Why is what Christians call the first part of their Bible so important?
2. Which of the several names for the first part of the Christian Bible (Old Testament, Hebrew Bible, Hebrew

Scriptures, Prime Testament, First Testament, Shared Testament) do you prefer and why?

3. What is the significance of the inclusion of religious texts from ancient Israel and early Judaism in the Christian Bible?

FOR FURTHER READING

Cunningham, Philip A. *Sharing the Scriptures.* Mahwah, N.J.: Paulist, 2003.

The Pontifical Biblical Commission. *The Jewish People and Their Sacred Scriptures in the Christian Bible.* Vatican City: Libreria Editrice Vaticana, 2002.

CHAPTER TWO

What's "In" and What's "Out"?

The previous chapter noted that there are some differences among Christian churches about what is to be included in the first part of the Christian Bible commonly known as the Old Testament. The Protestant collection is the smallest of all, containing thirty-nine books, and basically identical with the Hebrew Bible, although the rabbis count and arrange their books differently than do Protestant Christians. The Roman Catholic collection is somewhat larger, containing an additional seven books. The Greek Orthodox collection includes two more books plus an additional psalm and a prayer. The Ethiopian church has the largest collection of all—some eighty-one books. What is the reason for these differences? Who decided "what's in and what's out"? When were these decisions made and for what reason?

First of all, it is important to remember that during the "biblical period" there was no Bible. This may sound strange, but the Bible—as we know it—is a product of believers who lived much later than the people who composed the individual books that make up the Bible. For Roman Catholics the decision about what books make up the Bible was made only about 450 years ago—long after the books of the Bible were written. This decision on "what's in and what's out" was made by the Council of Trent on April 8, 1546, in large measure as a response to the Reformers who rejected certain books such as 2 Maccabees, which was used by Catholic theologians to support the doctrine of purgatory and prayers for the dead (see 2 Maccabees 12:43–45).

The Canon: A Text With Authority

The first book of the Bible to present itself as a written, authoritative text was the book of Deuteronomy:

> Then Moses wrote down this law, and gave it to the priests
> ….Moses commanded them: "Every seventh year…when
> all Israel comes to appear before the LORD…you shall read
> this law before all Israel in their hearing…so that they may
> hear and learn to fear the LORD…and to observe diligently all the words of this law.…" (31:9–12)

Deuteronomy, then, is responsible for the idea of a "Sacred Scripture." But the formation of the Scriptures as a collection of books took many centuries. The Bible is, after all, not a direct revelation of God to a single individual who carefully copied this revelation word for word. It is the record of the human response to the revelation of God to the ancient Israelite, early Jewish and early Christian communities. The word "Bible" comes from the Greek word for "books." The process that led from individual books such as Deuteronomy or Amos or Ecclesiastes to the collection we know as the Old Testament can only be partially reconstructed. We are familiar enough with the end product but how the Bible as a collection of sacred texts came to be is only partially understood.

The technical term for the collection of books accepted as authoritative by the community of believers is *canon*. This word is one of the few in English that is derived from a Semitic root *(qn)*, which appears in several Semitic languages including Hebrew. It passed into Greek as *kanna*, into Latin as *canna* and finally into English as *cane* and *canon*. The original meaning of the Semitic root was "reed," but eventually the word came to mean "something straight or firm." In the theological sphere, the word was used to speak of an article of faith or a biblical law. Saint Athanasius (d. 373) was the first to use the word "canon" to speak of the collection of the twenty-seven books of the New Testament. The word then gained wide currency and eventually came to include the books of the Old Testament as well.

In Jesus' day there was no agreement about the canon of Scripture among those who worshiped ancient Israel's ancestral deity. We should not think of early Judaism as if it had a structure similar to that of early Christianity, which early on developed a central authority to deal with controversial issues. For example, the book of Acts describes an assembly of "the apostles and the elders" to consider questions surrounding the admission of the gentiles into the Christian community (Acts 15). There was nothing similar in the Judaism of Jesus' day. Instead there were several ways those who served Israel's God expressed their beliefs and shaped their religious observance. For example, the Samaritans considered themselves true Israelites though the Jews did not. The Samaritans accepted only the Torah (the five books of Moses) as authoritative, rejecting the prophets and other religious texts produced by ancient Israel. The books outside the Torah were produced, or at least edited, in Judah. The people of Judah tended to see Israel's future as tied with the Davidic dynasty and the city of Jerusalem. The Samaritans were descendants of those who rejected this dynasty, so it is understandable that they would not embrace the prophetic literature.

Though the Sadducees were Jews, they, like the Samaritans, accepted only the Torah as authoritative. The Synoptic Gospels tell the story of a discussion between Jesus and some Sadducees about the resurrection of the dead (Matthew 22:23–33; Mark 12:18–27; Luke 20:27–40). The evangelists note that the Sadducees denied the resurrection (see Matthew 22:23). In trying to persuade them to believe in the resurrection of the dead, Jesus could not cite two explicit references to the resurrection in the Old Testament (Isaiah 26:19 and Daniel 12:2) because these came from books that the Sadducees did not accept as authoritative. That is the reason Jesus supports his argument with a citation from Exodus (3:6). Jesus uses this text to imply that Abraham, Isaac and Jacob were still living and this could only be possible if there were a resurrection. While the Sadducees may not have been persuaded, they could not fault Jesus' response because he met them on their own terms, citing what was for them an authoritative text.

The Pharisees, however, had a much wider canon. It included not only the Torah but also the prophets and the writings (a collection of miscellaneous religious texts). By the end of the first century A.D., this canon became stabilized into a collection of twenty-four books according to 4 Ezra 14:44–46. Among these twenty-four were the five Books of Moses (Genesis, Exodus, Leviticus, Numbers, Deuteronomy) and eight prophetic books divided into two subgroups (the Former Prophets [Joshua, Judges, Samuel and Kings] and the Latter Prophets [Isaiah, Jeremiah, Ezekiel and the Twelve]). In the prophetic collection, 1 and 2 Samuel were counted as a single book as were 1 and 2 Kings. The "Twelve" were the so-called "minor prophets" whose combined works are counted as one. The final collection (the Writings) included Ruth, Psalms, Job, Proverbs, Ecclesiastes, Song of Songs, Lamentations, Daniel, Esther, Ezra-Nehemiah and Chronicles. This is still the canon of the Jewish community today—sometimes called the "rabbinic canon."

Apparently, Jesus and the early Christians accepted the wider Pharisaic canon. There are several references to the "Law and the Prophets" (the first two parts of the Pharisaic canon) in the New Testament: Matthew 5:17; 7:12; 22:40; Luke 16:16; John 13:15; 24:14; and Romans 3:21. In one of the appearances of the Risen Jesus to the "eleven and their companions," Jesus reminds them of all he has taught them from "the law of Moses, the prophets, and the psalms" (Luke 24:44). The reference to the "psalms" may be an oblique reference to the third division of the Pharisaic canon. But some early Christians considered a few Jewish texts not found in the Pharisaic canon as authoritative. For example, Jude 1:14

cites a text from 1 Enoch and characterizes it as prophecy, though this book is not included among the prophetic collection of the Pharisees.

While 1 Enoch was not part of the Pharisaic canon, it was preserved and transmitted by another group of Jews, who called themselves "the sons of light." This was a group of priests who, because of a dispute with the temple authorities, left Jerusalem and moved to an area known as Qumran along the northwest shore of the Dead Sea to await their vindication. The community was wiped out during the First Jewish Revolt against Rome (A.D. 66–70), but a large collection of their religious texts was found in caves near their settlement beginning in 1948. This collection is known as the Dead Sea Scrolls. Among these scrolls were fragments from every book of the Hebrew Bible except the Book of Esther. Also included were several books like Sirach and 1 Enoch, which are not in the Hebrew Bible but apparently were considered important religious works by the people of Qumran. Whether the Qumran community considered works like Sirach and 1 Enoch to be on a par with the books that form the Pharisaic canon is not known. Still, it is clear that there were several "canons" among Jews of first century Palestine.

The Septuagint: The Old Testament in Greek

Many Jews living outside of Palestine wanted not only to maintain their identity as Jews, but they also wished to nourish their religious lives. One way to achieve these ends was through the reading and study of Jewish religious literature. In the Greek period (from the fourth to the first century B.C.), there was a large Jewish community in Egypt. Many

Jews settled in a city along Egypt's Mediterranean coast founded by Alexander the Great and named for himself: Alexandria. By the time of Jesus, one quarter of the city's population was Jewish. In fact, Alexandria with its more than one hundred thousand Jews was the largest Jewish city in the world—far ahead of Jerusalem itself. Already in the third century B.C., the Jewish community of Alexandria recognized the need for a Greek translation of the Torah since the Jews of the city spoke Greek and the ability to read and understand Hebrew was diminishing among them. By the first century, the Jews of Alexandria translated not only the entire Hebrew Bible into Greek but also produced additions to some books such as Esther and Daniel. The Alexandrian canon also included Jewish religious books originally written in Greek such as the Wisdom of Solomon and Greek translations of works originally written in Hebrew such as Ecclesiasticus (Sirach).

The name given to this Greek collection of Jewish religious literature is the *Septuagint,* which is often abbreviated with the Roman numerals LXX (70) since the word *septuagint* derives from the Latin word for "seventy." The name reflects the legend about the production of this collection. One Jewish tradition asserts that the Greek translation of the Hebrew Scriptures was accomplished in seventy days by seventy-two scholars (six from each of the twelve tribes). Though they worked separately, when they came together and compared their translations, they were found to agree word for word. This story is clearly an attempt to show the miraculous nature of the collection's production so as to provide the translation with a divine warrant since there was no precedent for translating the Hebrew Scriptures into another language. The Septuagint was an innovation that needed justification for a people who lived by what they believed to be divinely determined tradition.

The Roman Catholic Canon

The Septuagint played an important role in the early church since the greater portion of the first Christian community was Greek-speaking. The New Testament was originally produced in Greek though Jesus and his disciples were Jews from Palestine. When the authors of the New Testament cite texts from the Old Testament, they often cited the Septuagint version instead of attempting their own translation of the text from Hebrew. Among the most significant instances of this phenomenon is Matthew's citation of Isaiah 7:14 at the conclusion of the story of Joseph's dream in Matthew 1:23. Matthew purposely cites the Septuagint version of the Isaian text because it reads : "…the virgin shall conceive and bear a son…" while the Hebrew reads: "…the young woman is with child and shall bear a son:…" Matthew chose to use the Septuagint reading because he wanted to assert that the Christian belief in the virgin birth of Jesus has warrant in prophetic tradition.

When the Old Testament was first translated into Latin, the translators did not use the Hebrew text as the basis of their Latin rendition but instead used the Septuagint. Later, when Saint Jerome produced his Latin translation of the Old Testament in the fourth century, there was some strong resistance to it at first because he used the Hebrew Scriptures rather than the Septuagint as the basis for his new Latin translation, which became known as the Vulgate. Jerome's Vulgate did not achieve wide acceptance in the church until after his death. Eventually, the Vulgate became the version of the Old Testament for the Catholic church as decreed by the Council of Trent. The texts that comprise the Vulgate's collection of Old Testament books have become the canon of the Old Testament for Catholics. Jerome's translation has been revised several times, most recently in 1979. This New Vulgate enjoys the preeminence once accorded to Jerome's translation. For example, the Vatican document *Liturgiam authenticam* requires that the lectionary readings to be used during the Eucharist reflect a clear correspondence to the New Vulgate's rendering of the text to be read.

The Roman Catholic canon of the Old Testament, then, includes the Law, Prophets and Writings of the rabbinic canon plus additions to the books of Esther and Daniel as well as seven books that are found in the Septuagint but not in the rabbinic Bible: Tobit, Judith, Wisdom, Ecclesiasticus (Sirach), Baruch and 1 and 2 Maccabees. The canon of Protestant churches is identical to the rabbinic canon; however, the order of both the Catholic and Protestant Old Testament collections follows that of the Septuagint rather than the rabbinic Bible. Instead of arranging the books in sub-collections as the rabbis do (Torah, Prophets, Writings), Christian Bibles organize their Old Testament collection into historical books, poetic books and prophetic books—giving the collection a type of "past, present and future" orientation. The significance of these two different arrangements is clear when the ending of the rabbinic canon is compared with that of the Christian canon.

The Last Word

The last book of the rabbinic canon is 2 Chronicles. This book concludes by reproducing the decree of Cyrus, who urged the Jews to return to Jerusalem from exile in Babylon and join in rebuilding the temple: "The LORD, the God of heaven, has…charged me to build him a house at Jerusalem …. Whoever is among you of all his people, may the LORD his God be with him! Let him go up" (2 Chronicles 36:23). The last word Jews read in their Bible is a call to return to Jerusalem, which engenders the hope that Jerusalem will be restored as the place where God will dwell on earth and where God will receive the worship of all peoples.

The last book of the Christian Old Testament is the book of Malachi, so the final words of the Old Testament that Christians read are:

> Lo, I will send you the prophet Elijah before the great and terrible day of the LORD comes. He will turn the hearts of parents to their children and the hearts of children to their parents, so that I will not come and strike the land with a curse. (Malachi 4:5–6)

The Gospels identify John the Baptist as the Elijah whom God sent to prepare the way for Jesus. Luke has the angel who appeared to Zechariah cite the Malachi text in describing the future of the son that was to be born to Zechariah and Elizabeth (see Luke 1:17). The last words that Christians read in their Old Testament point to the mission of the Baptist, who announced the coming of Jesus—"the great and terrible day of the Lord."

The arrangement of the Christian canon of the Old Testament has set a pattern for the Christian appropriation of its scriptural heritage from ancient Israel and early Judaism—a pattern of promise and fulfillment. This is the pattern that the liturgy uses for the most part. For example, the readings from the New Testament are semi-continuous while the reading from the Old Testament usually is related in some way to the theme of the Gospel reading. Consider the Old Testament and gospel lessons for the twenty-fifth Sunday of Ordinary Time in each of the three Sunday lectionary cycles.

In Year A the gospel lesson is the parable of the laborers in the vineyard (Matthew 20:1–16). When those hired first complain that they were paid as much as those hired toward the end of the working day, the owner of the vineyard asks the disgruntled laborers if they are "envious because I am generous. So the last will be first and the first will be last" (verses 15–16). The Old Testament lesson is taken from Isaiah 55:6–9 which contains the saying "…my thoughts are not your thoughts, nor are your ways my ways…says the LORD" (verse 8)—a clear allusion to the point of the parable.

The gospel lesson for year B is the second prediction of the passion (Mark 9:30–37) while the Old Testament lesson is taken from Wisdom 2:12, 17–20, which are the words of evil people plotting against a righteous person: "Let us lie in wait for the righteous man…"

The parable of the dishonest manager (Luke 16:1–13) is the gospel lesson in year C: "I have decided what to do so that, when I am dismissed as manager, people may welcome me into their homes.…" The Old Testament lesson is Amos's condemnation of the avarice of the rich (8:4–7): "Hear this, you that trample on the needy...".

In each of these instances, the Old Testament lesson is not allowed to stand on its own, but is read to enhance the congregation's understanding and appreciation of the Gospel's message. While there is nothing inherently wrong about this approach, the Old Testament has much more to offer were its own theological perspectives and moral values allowed to speak for themselves. The rest of this book will attempt to do just that—by looking at Old Testament motifs that, at first reading, seem to be problematic or difficult for the Christian readers. The purpose of this book is to help Christian readers find in the Old Testament what the Israelites and Jews have found there for millennia:

Your word is a lamp to my feet
and a light to my path.
(Psalm 119:105)

QUESTIONS FOR REFLECTION
1. What is the role of "canon" in communities of faith?
2. In what sense is it true to say that the Bible is the creation of the synagogue and church?
3. What role did the Septuagint play in the formation of the Christian canon?
4. What are some of the differences between the arrangement of books in the rabbinic canon and in the Christian canons of the Old Testament?
5. What is the importance of the Vulgate for the canon of the Old Testament in the Roman Catholic church?

6. How does the church use the Old Testament canon in the Liturgy of the Word?

FOR FURTHER READING

Barton, John. *Holy Writings, Sacred Text: The Canon in Early Christianity.* Louisville: Westminster John Knox, 1998.

Beckwith, Roger T. *The Old Testament Canon of the New Testament Church and Its Background in Early Judaism.* Grand Rapids: Eerdmans, 1985.

Brueggemann, Walter. *The Creative Word: Canon as a Model for Biblical Education.* Philadelphia: Fortress, 1982.

Seitz, Christopher. *Word Without End: The Old Testament as Abiding Theological Witness.* Grand Rapids: Eerdmans, 1998.

CHAPTER THREE

What Does the Old Testament Say About God?

Nowhere is the distance between the Bible and its modern Christian readers more apparent than in what the Old Testament says about God. In an age that has witnessed two world wars and many regional conflicts, genocides and mass murders, terrorism and violence, and the destruction effected by two atomic bombs, all sane people recoil at the specter of the human suffering brought about by conflicts between people, thus the Old Testament image of God as a warrior appears not merely as a relic of another age but as a perversion of the Christian message. Equally difficult for some is Jesus' addressing God as father. Though it uses the imagery of intimacy, it also shaped the New Testament's image of God in almost exclusively masculine terms, leaving women to wonder how they reflect the "image and likeness of God." The Bible also speaks of a God who is both near and far, close and distant, and who is the only source of hope. What then are readers today to think of the God of the Bible?

Yahweh Sabaoth

A good place to begin is with the name "Yahweh"—the proper name of ancient Israel's patron deity. Every one of ancient Israel's neighbors had its own national god: the Philistines had Dagon, the Moabites Chemosh, and the Babylonians Marduk. Israel's God had to have a proper name to help the Israelites distinguish their God from the gods of their neighbors. Israel's basic confession of faith in their God calls this God by name:

> Listen, Israel: Yahweh our God is the one, the only Yahweh. (Deuteronomy 6:4)

The meaning of the name Yahweh is not absolutely clear, though the name probably was meant to evoke God's power and presence.

The people of Israel acclaimed Yahweh whom they remembered as the God who freed them from slavery in Egypt and gave them a land (Deuteronomy 26:5–10). The name Yahweh was sometimes associated with another word to make a fuller title. One of the most frequently used and most problematic of these compound names is "Yahweh Sabaoth," commonly translated as "the Lord of Hosts." The "hosts" are the heavenly and earthly armies that Israel's God uses to protect it. It is possible to translate "Yahweh Sabaoth" as "militant Yahweh," for the title envisions God as a divine warrior. The significance of this title becomes clear in the stories about Israel's wars with the Philistines, with whom Israel was contending for dominance in Canaan. After a stinging defeat the Israelites, at the direction of the elders, brought the ark of the covenant on which Yahweh Sabaoth was enthroned from Shiloh to their camp (1 Samuel 4:4). The purpose of this act was to bring Yahweh's power into play on Israel's side (the effort was ultimately unsuccessful, however). In another story, the young David addresses Goliath: "You come to me with sword and spear and javelin; but I come to you in the name of the LORD of hosts [Yahweh Sabaoth], the God of the armies of Israel" (1 Samuel 17:45).

Though this title occurs over 250 times in the books of the Old Testament, it is unevenly distributed among these books. For example, it never appears in the Pentateuch. It occurs fifty-three times in the fourteen chapters of Zechariah but not at all in the much longer book of Ezekiel. The distribution is sometimes uneven within individual books. "Yahweh Sabaoth" occurs fifty-six times in Isaiah 1 through 39, but only six times in Isaiah 40 through 55 and not at all in Isaiah 56 through 66. This shows that ancient Israel used this title for God when it was necessary to affirm that God was victorious over the forces arrayed against Israel. This title, then, is not a description of divinity as much as it is an act of faith in Israel's future—a future that was under almost a continuous threat from political and military powers in the ancient Near East.

Does the militancy implicit in this title suggest that the people of ancient Israel understood their God as engaging in violence and commanding violence against Israel's enemies? Does this mean that the Bible makes violent retribution a divine prerogative, or that God approves of violence done in God's name? Certainly violence pervades the Bible from beginning to end: God virtually destroys the created world in a great flood because of human wickedness (Genesis 6:5). The books of Joshua and Judges have the Israelite armies slaughtering the indigenous population of Canaan as an act of devotion to God (see Joshua 6:17). The book of Maccabees approves the killing of unfaithful Jews and the making of war against the armies of Antiochus IV (1 Maccabees 2:15–28). Even women take up the sword. Deborah encourages Barak and the armies of several tribes to fight against the Canaanites (Judges 4—5), and Judith kills an enemy general with her own hand (Judges 13:6–9). Jesus too resorts to violence as he "cleanses" the temple (Matthew 21:12–17). In the parable of the wicked tenants, Jesus implies that God will answer violence with violence (Matthew 21:33–43). The final act in the Last Judgment will be the casting of those not found in the book of life into the "lake of fire" (Revelation 20:14).

The world that witnessed the production of the Bible was a world of violence. The Israelite tribes emerged in the central highlands of Canaan in a time of significant upheaval throughout the eastern Mediterranean world. Saul, Israel's first king, committed suicide after his army suffered a terrible defeat. Several of his successors in both Judah and Israel were assassinated. One died by his own hand; another died in battle and two died in exile. The Assyrians dismembered the kingdom of Israel and absorbed its territory into their provincial system. The Babylonians did the same to the kingdom of Judah and took many of Judah's leadership class into exile. The Persians allowed Jewish exiles to return, but Judah was reduced to the city of Jerusalem and its immediate environs. The Greeks replaced the Persians. Though the

Maccabees led a successful revolution against Greek rule, Judah's real independence lasted for about eighty years before Rome brought Judah into its orbit. The Romans mistakenly believed that Jesus constituted a threat to their rule and so executed him. The first Christian community was harassed by a small clique of Jews who were offended by their assertions about Jesus (Acts 8:5). Some early Christian leaders were executed for their testimony (Acts 7; 12:2). It was not long before most Christians had to live in fear. Portions of the New Testament were written to encourage Christians who were persecuted because of their belief in Jesus.

The Bible could not ignore the agrarian experience of its people, thus it could not ignore the violence that was also part of their experience. Just as the prophet identified Yahweh as the one who gave Israel "the grain, the new wine and the oil" (Hosea 2:8), so it was natural to identify Yahweh as the Lord of Israel's armies, who drove out the nations from the land. Just as the nations had their gods who fought for them, so Israel had its patron deity: Yahweh. For the people of antiquity, nothing happened by chance—all was the result of actions by the gods.

By the time the New Testament was written, the territory of the former Israelite kingdoms had been occupied by foreign invaders for eight hundred years—except for the time of an independent Jewish kingdom following the Maccabean revolt (142–63 B.C.). The occupation was often brutal and debilitating. Some Jews came to believe that this world was not to witness the triumph of divine justice. There was to be one final conflict between God and the powers of evil in which God will emerge completely victorious. This is the worldview of the New Testament generally and of the book of Revelation in particular. God's final and decisive victory will take place at the end of the age when God will utterly defeat all the powers of evil.

A serious theological problem may arise for the readers of Joshua, Judges, Revelation and other biblical texts that describe acts of violence done in the name of or at the behest of God. Often readers detach these stories from the lived experience that gave them shape. Two consequences commonly follow from such readings. Evangelical and conservative readers assume that God not only permits war and the human suffering associated with it but, at times, requires believers to take up arms. For example, during the American Civil War most soldiers on both sides were sincere Christians who believed that they were doing God's bidding: for the armies of the North, the war became a crusade to free the slaves; for the soldiers from the South, it was a crusade to preserve God-given rights.

In our day, among the most vocal opponents of nuclear disarmament are conservative Christians who see the West locked in a battle with non-Christian forces intent on destroying Christian civilization. On the other hand, more liberal Christians oppose war, and many consider the biblical stories about the wars of ancient Israel as examples of a primitive and unsophisticated religion whose perspectives are not only irrelevant but dangerous today. The Bible's attitude toward war and violence undercuts the whole of its moral vision that appears to be too closely tied to the experience of another age.

The Roman Catholic liturgy uses the phrase "Yahweh Sabaoth" in the acclamation following the preface to the Eucharistic Prayer. That acclamation begins with a paraphrase of Isaiah 6:3: "Holy, holy, holy is the LORD of Hosts [Yahweh Sabaoth]; the whole earth is full of his glory." Isaiah 6 recounts the prophet's vision of God in the Jerusalem temple where God was worshiped as Yahweh Sabaoth. That title served to underscore Yahweh's "power and might" as the patron deity of the Judahite national state. The contemporary Christian use of this title carries with it none of the political overtones that were characteristic of its use in the worship of the temple. Today the implication of the title's usage centers on God's cosmic power as Creator—an emphasis also present in many of the Old Testament passages that speak of Israel's God as Yahweh Sabaoth.

The use of the phrase "Lord God of power and might" in the liturgy is a point of contact with our ancestors in the faith who worshiped their God using the very same title. At some time, however, the ancient Israelites stopped pronouncing the name Yahweh and began to use titles and circumlocutions in referring to their God. The precise time this happened and the circumstances that led to it are unclear, but by Jesus' day the Jews held the proper name of their God in such reverential awe that this name was uttered only once each year by the high priest who entered the most sacred part of the temple to intercede for his people on the Day of Atonement.

In reading the biblical text or using biblical prayers, it became customary among the Jews to substitute the Hebrew word *Adonai* (Lord) for *Yahweh*. To insure that the divine name would not be spoken even by mistake, scribes who copied the sacred text attached the vowels for *adonai* to the consonants of *Yahweh*. (Those who produced the King James Version of the Bible in the early seventeenth century were unaware of this and rendered the divine name as *Jehovah*, which is certainly not the way the divine name was pronounced!) It has become customary in most Christian Bibles to use the word *Lord* in small capitals—LORD—whenever the Hebrew text has the divine name. This is to respect the sensitivity of religious Jews regarding the custom of never pronouncing God's name. The editors of the *Jerusalem Bible* chose not to follow this practice; however, in the preface to their translation, the editors advise readers to make the customary substitution whenever reading the text aloud. Unfortunately, some Catholics have not followed this advice and the use of the divine name has crept into usage not only in public reading but also in contemporary hymns. Respect for traditional Jewish practice suggests that Christians ought to avoid pronouncing the Name of God. The customs of Judaism regarding the divine name are a rebuke to any Christian who does not show proper reverence in speaking about God or in using God's name or the name of Jesus.

The God of Peace

Of course, the Bible's moral vision also embraces reconciliation and peace. Some of most stirring words and engaging images engender thoughts of peace:

For a child has been born for us,
  a son given to us;
authority rests upon his shoulders;
  and he is named
Wonderful Counselor, Mighty God,
  Everlasting Father, Prince of Peace.
(Isaiah 9:6)

He shall judge between many peoples,
  and shall arbitrate between strong nations far away;
they shall beat their swords into plowshares,
  and their spears into pruning hooks;
nation shall not lift up sword against nation,
  neither shall they learn war any more;
but they shall sit under their own vines and under their
    own fig trees,
  and no one shall make them afraid;
  for the mouth of the LORD of hosts has spoken.
(Micah 4:3–4)

And suddenly there was with the angel a multitude of the
heavenly host praising God and saying,
  "Glory to God in the highest heaven,
    and on earth peace among those whom he favors!"
(Luke 2:13–14)

The psalmist encourages Yahweh's worshipers, "Depart from evil, and do good; / seek peace, and pursue it" (Psalm 34:14). Believers will look forward to the one who will proclaim peace: "Look! On the mountains the feet of one who brings good tidings, who proclaims peace!" (Nahum 1:15).

The word "peace" appears in almost every book of the New Testament. Certainly the teaching and practice of Jesus lie behind this usage. Jesus dismissed those he had healed with the words "Go in peace" (see Mark 5:34), and he wished his followers to live in peace with each other (Mark 9:50). Peace is Jesus' parting gift to his disciples (John 14:27). Still, peace involves more than an absence of conflict: "Do not think that I have come to bring peace to the earth; I have not come to bring peace, but a sword" (Matthew 10:34). Jesus' claim of absolute loyalty will create divisions within families where peace should reign. The disciple's commitment to Jesus takes precedence even over the sacred commitments that family members have to each other. Jesus wished that every disciple be known as a "child of peace" (see Luke 10:6), and the epistles, too, emphasize that peacemaking is to be among the first priorities of Jesus' disciples (Romans 12:18; 14:19; Hebrews 12:14; 1 Peter 3:11). Peacemaking is at the heart of the biblical tradition. The Bible offers no higher calling to the believer than to be a "child of peace."

Our Father

The prayer Jesus taught presents an even more intimate view of God. In what has become known as "the Lord's Prayer" (Matthew 6:9–13), Jesus has his disciples address God as "Father," just as he does. This usage suggests a closeness that characterizes the believers' relationship with God, but it also led to the New Testament's almost exclusive use of masculine images in speaking about God. The exceptions are in

Luke's Gospel: the parable of the lost coin (Luke 15:8–10), the parable of the yeast (Luke 13:20–21) and the parable of the unjust judge (Luke 18:2–8). The New Testament's reliance on masculine imagery to speak of God has led to a similar reliance in contemporary Christian worship. An increasing number of believers today find the exclusive use of masculine metaphors in addressing or speaking about God to be troublesome. They feel that this impoverishes the language of prayer and theology. What are we to make of the Bible's almost exclusive reliance on male language in speaking about God? Many Catholics suggest that in speaking and writing and especially in the liturgy, we use non-gender specific language when referring to God. How does this jibe with the biblical witness? If Jesus speaks about God as "father," doesn't this settle the issue? How can we legitimately speak of God as "mother"?

The people of ancient Israel thought of Yahweh as a male deity though the Old Testament does occasionally use feminine imagery in speaking about God. The Isaianic tradition portrays God as a mother (Isaiah 42:14; 49:15; 66:12b–13). That same tradition also addresses God as father (Isaiah 63:16; 64:8). Psalm 2 speaks of Judah's king as God's son. The notion that God was the father of Israel is commonplace in the Bible (Exodus 4:22; Deuteronomy 14:1; 32:6; Hosea 11:1; Jeremiah 3:4, 19; 31:9; Psalm 103:13). But for the most part, the Hebrew Bible uses other images to suggest the intimacy between God and the worshiper. The prophet Hosea suggests that God's love for Israel is like that of a husband for his wife (Hosea 3:1).

But it was the political sphere that served to provide ancient Israel's theologians with what became the most fundamental metaphor in speaking about the love that ought to bind Israel and God. The vocabulary of international treaties in the ancient Near East included the word *hesed,* a word that is notoriously difficult to translate. It describes the attitude of commitment and freedom that is to characterize people in a covenant relationship. The Bible uses *hesed* over 250 times to speak about the love, commitment and loyalty that was to give shape to Israel's relationship with God.

Mark's version of Jesus' prayer in the Garden of Gethsemane has Jesus address God as *Abba* (Mark 14:36), an Aramaic form for "the father" (not "daddy" as sometimes suggested). Paul's use of this term (Romans 8:15; Galatians 4:6) suggests that some Christian communities adopted Jesus' usage as their own. Though early Jews did think of God as the father of individual believers (see Sirach 23:1; Wisdom 2:16), there is no evidence that before Jesus' day Jews addressed prayers to God using the Aramaic form *abba,* so the use of that word in Christian prayer is a unique development. This development likely was meant to underscore the intimacy that exists between God and the Christian believer—a notion based on Jesus' teaching and the example of his own prayer. An additional motivation for the first Christians to use the father metaphor in prayer was the title *pater patriae* ("father of the fatherland") claimed by the Roman emperors. Addressing God as father was an act of resistance to the empire that forbade the practice of the Christian faith.

The challenge for the church today is to find other

metaphors that avoid the exclusive use of masculine images while still capturing the closeness between God and believers that the father metaphor suggests. An obvious possibility is the mother image, which the book of Isaiah uses several times.

> For thus says the LORD:
> I will extend prosperity to her like a river,
>> and the wealth of the nations like an overflowing
>> stream;
> and you shall nurse and be carried on her arm,
>> and dandled on her knees.
> As a mother comforts her child,
>> so I will comfort you;
>> you shall be comforted in Jerusalem.
> (Isaiah 66:12–13)

It is not necessary to abandon the father metaphor to insure that mother imagery, which also has biblical warrant, finds its way into the prayer and discourse of believers. The mother's special role in the birthing and nurturing of her children accents the intimacy between God and believers in a way that the image of God as father does not. It also emphasizes the depth, persistence and compassion evident in the relationship of mother and child:

> Can a woman forget her nursing child,
>> or show no compassion for the child of her womb?
> Even these may forget,
>> yet I will not forget you.
> (Isaiah 49:15)

In Psalm 51:3 (verse 1, ET), the psalmist asks for forgiveness by calling on God's compassion. The Hebrew word for "compassion" *(rhmym)* is derived from the word for "womb" *(rhm)*. The psalmist is asking God to act as a mother would act toward her child. What this suggests is that God's presence and action in human experience is mediated by the experience unique to both men and women. It is important to call upon the range of human experience to have an adequate appreciation of the way God is present in human experience.

The God Who Dances

The problem we face in using the range of human experience in speaking of God is the strangeness of feminine images of the divine. The exclusive use of masculine images for God in the language of prayer and theology makes addressing God as "mother" sound discomforting, though intellectually one may admit that such imagery is legitimate. God, after all, is beyond gender, and both the masculine and feminine metaphors that people may use to speak about God portray God in ways that human beings can understand and appreciate. But are there limits to the kinds of metaphors that we are willing to use to speak about God? How much of our experience can contribute to our God-language? Are there ways of speaking about God that can open up new ways of appreciating the presence of God in our lives? Does the Bible offer any guidance here?

Actually, the Bible is quite daring in its use of metaphors for the Divinity. For example, while there are problems with the Hebrew vocabulary of Zephaniah 3:17, the passage appears to present God as singing and dancing when the exile of the Jews will end and they return to Jerusalem. The *New Jerusalem Bible* makes this explicit as it renders this verse as:

> Yahweh your God is there with you,
> the warrior-Savior.
> He will rejoice over you with a happy song,
> he will renew you by his love,
> he will dance with shouts of joy for you.

Dancing was a part of ancient Near Eastern worship, and ancient Israel made it part of its liturgy as well (see Exodus 15:20–21; Judges 21:19–21; 2 Samuel 6:5). But music, singing and dancing were also ways that people expressed their joy at happy occasions. Zephaniah does not hesitate to portray God as reacting to the people's return to Jerusalem by joining in the activity that the people themselves used to express their happiness at coming home. This metaphor suggests an intimacy that modern believers rarely associate with the God described in the Old Testament. The book of Zephaniah displays no illusions about the failures of God's people and the judgment that will come. Still, like all the prophets, Zephaniah does not believe that judgment is God's last word to Israel. He envisions a future in which God will join the people assembled for worship in festive singing and dancing.

Sometimes Christians find reading the Old Testament difficult because they find that the God portrayed on its pages is not the same God that Jesus preaches about in the New Testament. The God whom Jesus proclaims is the God revealed in the pages of the Law and the Prophets. The God of the New Testament can be as harsh and unforgiving as the God of the Old Testament.

If any of you put a stumbling block before one of these little ones who believe in me, it would be better for you if a great millstone were hung around your neck and you were thrown into the sea. (Mark 9:42)

...whoever blasphemes against the Holy Spirit will not be forgiven. (Luke 11:10b)

There will be weeping and gnashing of teeth when you see Abraham and Isaac and Jacob and all the prophets in the kingdom of God, and you yourselves thrown out. (Luke 13:28)

Of course, the God of the Old Testament can be as merciful and loving as the God of the New Testament:

The LORD is merciful and gracious,
    slow to anger and abounding in steadfast love.
(Psalm 103:8)

I [God] led them with cords of human kindness,
    with bands of love.
I was to them like those
    who lift infants to their cheeks.
(Hosea 11:4)

Contrasting the God of the Old Testament with the God of the New Testament is a futile exercise. They are one and the same. The God of Jesus is the God who sings and dances with those who have come home.

The God Beyond Calculation
As appealing as the image of a singing and dancing God may be, ancient Israel's wisdom tradition depicts a God whose pres-

ence in human experience is much more elusive. Israel's sages spoke about a God who is beyond human calculation and understanding. In reflecting on our experience of God, do we recognize the mystery that is the Divine? How does the Bible challenge us to recognize the fallibility of our insights into the Divine? More effectively than any other biblical writers, the sages conveyed the mystery of the Divine in Israel's life:

> Can you find out the deep things of God?
>> Can you find out the limit of the Almighty?
> It is higher than heaven—what can you do?
>> Deeper than Sheol—what can you know?
> (Job 11:7–8)
>
> Surely God is great, and we do not know him....
> (Job 36:26a)

The book of Proverbs displays a certain optimism about the possibility of mastering life, yet it repeatedly cautions that God is beyond human reckoning: "The human mind plans the way, / but the LORD directs the steps" (Proverbs 16:9). Still, the sages teach that there is a fundamental order to the world—an order that has been determined by God. They believe that human beings are to discern that order and live in conformity with it though they recognized the relativity of their insights—a relativity that follows from any human attempt to comprehend the Divine:

> No wisdom, no understanding, no counsel,
>> can avail against the LORD.
> (Proverbs 21:30)

This is brought out most dramatically in the book of Job. Job finds all the claims of a divinely established order in the world contradicted by his experience. He exclaims that a return to the primordial chaos would be better than the so-called divine order in creation (Job 3:3–10). God's reply to Job's complaints describes the grandeur of creation and implies that Job does not know what he is asking for when he calls for the world to return to chaos (Job 38:1—42:6). When Job begs God to help him understand his plight, God rebuffs the innocent sufferer by asserting that he could never understand any explanation that God may give. Only divine wisdom can grasp the ways of God. They are simply beyond human comprehension.

The writer of Ecclesiastes, the "Teacher" Qoheleth, expends all his energy in trying to grasp the mystery of God, but concludes that God has made it impossible for human beings to accomplish this task—despite the divine impetus for the human quest to understand the ways of God:

> I have seen the business that God has given to everyone to be busy with. He has made everything suitable for its time; moreover he has put a sense of past and future into their minds, yet they cannot find out what God has done from the beginning to the end. (Ecclesiastes 3:10–11)

Qoheleth's advice to those experiencing the absence of the Divine is to enjoy life (Ecclesiastes 3:12; 9:7–10) because the simple pleasures of life are God's gift to human beings.

Other of ancient Israel's sages, however, see their quest for wisdom as at least partially fulfilling the human longing for the divine. Wisdom, after all, is the firstborn of all creatures and was with God as God created the world (Proverbs 8:22–31). Sirach suggested that wisdom was to be found in the Torah of Moses (Sirach 24:23) so that obedience to the Torah was the infallible way to wisdom and God. The wise, then, affirm that our experience of God is, at best, indirect. They suggest that an authentic experience of the divine may be had in the search for wisdom—a wisdom that is most pre-eminently evident in the Torah.

The Lord Alone

"Hear, O Israel: The LORD is our God; the LORD alone" (Deuteronomy 6:4). Religious Jews utter this confession of faith several times each day. These were the last words of many who died in the Holocaust. This confession embodies the heritage of monotheism that Judaism, Christianity and Islam received from the religion of ancient Israel. But the formulation of this confession, which takes up only six words in Hebrew, took many centuries. How did monotheism develop among the people of ancient Israel? What led them to see God as one?

The first Israelites honored the Lord as their patron deity who gave them the land, which was their means of survival. They believed that God had promised this land to their ancestors Abraham, Isaac and Jacob. The fulfillment of this promise involved freeing the descendants of Jacob from slavery in Egypt and guiding them into the land of Canaan (see Deuteronomy 26:5–9). But the Israelites assumed that each nation had its own patron deity. Their neighbors the Moabites had Chemosh and the Ammonites had Molech.

The Canaanites had Baal, who was the main rival for Israel's loyalty during most of the biblical period.

The Israelites were also drawn to the worship of Baal, in part, because of the geographic and climatic peculiarities of the land of Israel. This land was without a major river system that could make irrigation possible. The water for their fields and animals had to come in the form of rain. When the rainfall was insufficient, life was difficult. When there were several years of meager rainfall, famine was the result. To relieve their anxiety about having enough rain each year many Israelites turned to the worship of Baal, a god associated with the storms that brought rain. The Israelites believed that the Lord had originally come from the southern wilderness—a barren and dry land (see Habakkuk 3:3). While they were grateful for the land that the Lord gave them, the Israelites believed that their survival on that land required that they turn to Baal, who would bring them the rain they needed. The prophets, especially Elijah (see 1 Kings 18) and Hosea, tried to help the Israelites recognize that it was the Lord—not Baal—who brought the rain that made the land fruitful.

Isaiah 40—55 signals the triumph of the "Lord alone" movement in ancient Israel. This triumph came, in part, because of Israel's encounter with the Persians. It was the Persian king Cyrus, whom Isaiah acclaimed as the Lord's anointed [messiah], who defeated the Babylonians and encouraged the Jewish exiles to return to Jerusalem and rebuild the temple to the Lord (see 2 Chronicles 36:23). Persian religion was based on the belief in two competing divinities who were locked in an eternal battle: Ahura Mazda, the god of light, and Ahriman, the god of darkness. The Persians believed that the gods of other nations were local manifestations of Ahura Mazda, so they encouraged the worship of national deities like the Lord. Isaiah 45:5, however, asserts that the Lord alone is God and claims that it was the Lord who gave Cyrus victory over the Babylonians:

> I am the LORD, and there is no other;
>> besides me there is no god.
> I arm you [Cyrus], though you do not know me.
> (Isaiah 45:5)

The great theological problem that flows from monotheism is the presence and power of evil in the world. Ancient Near Eastern peoples explained evil in the world as a consequence of conflict between the gods. The Persians blamed Ahriman for evil. By asserting that the Lord was the only God, the prophet had to deal with the problem of evil—something that he recognized as he has the Lord assert:

> I form light and create darkness,
>> I make weal and create woe;
>> I the LORD do all these things.
> (Isaiah 45:7)

Allegory and Theology

The differences between our modern understanding of God and the ancient view is clearly apparent as it is when ancient Israel speaks of its God. Marcion, a second-century Christian theologian, responded to this "otherness" by rejecting the Old Testament entirely. Indeed, Marcion rejected a good part of the New Testament as well, accepting only the letters of Paul and a version of Luke that omitted the infancy narrative, all references to John the Baptist and all citations of Old Testament prophecy. The church disavowed Marcion's approach. It appropriated the Scriptures of the Jewish community because it recognized that the God of Jesus was the God of these Scriptures. The church's appropriation of the Jewish Scriptures does not solve the problem of the "otherness" of those Scriptures. Most early and medieval theologians and preachers tried to solve the problem by allegorizing the Old Testament. Another approach was to consider the Old Testament a primitive and theologically unsophisticated collection of books whose concept of God was incomplete, requiring the revelation of Jesus Christ to bring to perfection God's revelation to ancient Israel.

An alternative to these approaches is for the Christian reader today to engage the biblical text as a partner in dialogue. The reader of these ancient texts must become contemporaneous with them, trying to hear them as those who first heard them did. It is not easy to bridge the cultural, linguistic and historical gaps that exist between the biblical period and our own, but it is certainly possible. Reading with a sympathetic and understanding eye is the way to begin. Once readers immerse themselves in the world of the text, identifying with its first readers, they are in a position to make the text resonate with believers today. These two steps are complementary and necessary. Without any effort to make the text contemporaneous with today's issues, reading the Bible becomes either an exercise in reconstructing the religion of ancient Israel, or the text becomes so vague that readers too easily find their own theological and social views.

The images that the Bible uses to speak about God come from the lives and experiences of real people. Getting to know and appreciate these people, their struggles, failures, hopes and beliefs is a more productive way to read the Bible than to look for abstract doctrines. This is nowhere more evident than when trying to appreciate how the Bible speaks about God. The God of the Bible is Yahweh Sabaoth, who protects Israel when its existence is threatened; Father and Mother, caring for God's children; the God who dances with joy over the repentance and return of those who have strayed; the elusive God who is always beyond our calculation; and the only God—the only source of hope.

QUESTIONS FOR REFLECTION

1. What Old Testament image of God do you find most engaging? What Old Testament image of God do you find most disturbing?
2. Why is the imagery we use in speaking about God so important? How can the Old Testament broaden our horizons regarding the imagery we use to speak about God?
3. What is the significance of ancient Israel having a proper name for its God?
4. How does the Old Testament show that God's presence is always elusive?
5. What are some of the consequences in believing in one God?

FOR FURTHER READING

Clements, Ronald E. *Old Testament Theology: A Fresh Approach.* Atlanta: John Knox, 1979.

Johnson, Elizabeth A. *She Who Is: The Mystery of God in Feminist Theological Discourse.* New York: Crossroad, 1992.

Lang, Bernhard. *Monotheism and the Prophetic Minority: An Essay in Biblical History and Sociology.* Sheffield, England: Almond Press, 1983.

Levenson, Jon. *Sinai and Zion: An Entry into the Jewish Bible.* San Francisco: Harper and Row, 1987.

Terrien, Samuel. *The Elusive Presence: Toward a New Biblical Theology.* San Francisco: Harper and Row, 1978.

CHAPTER FOUR

Israel—The Chosen People?

As challenging as the Old Testament's ways of speaking about God is the self-image of the people who produced and transmitted this Testament. These Scriptures are suffused with the notion that Israel is God's chosen people. Some contemporary Christian readers ask themselves, "Aren't all people God's people?" How can one nation claim special status? Aren't such claims irrelevant given God's revelation in Jesus Christ, because of whom the distinction between Jew and Gentile has become of no significance?

Certainly, this is an important motif in Paul's letters (see Romans 3:9; 10:12; 1 Corinthians 1:24; 12:13; Galatians 3:28; Colossians 3:11). Still, the Gospels leave the reader with the impression that Jesus saw his ministry as directed solely to Israel: "I was sent only to the lost sheep of the house of Israel" (Matthew 5:24). Jesus orders the twelve to follow his example: "Go nowhere among the Gentiles, and enter no town of the Samaritans, but go rather to the lost sheep of the house of Israel" (Matthew 10:5).

It is not surprising, then, that the first crisis in the church's life was over the question of the inclusion of the gentiles into the Christian community. Some Christians wanted to limit the mission of the church to the Jews. They saw the confessing of Jesus as the Messiah and living according to the ideals of the gospel as a new way of being a Jew. Others were willing to admit gentiles into the community of those who confessed Jesus as the Messiah as long as these converts became observant Jews. Paul objected strenuously (Galatians 2:11, 14). He asserted that it was God's will to bring the gentiles to salvation by faith in Jesus—not through Jewish religious observance:

> For we hold that a person is justified by faith apart from works prescribed by the law. Or is God the God of Jews only? Is he not the God of Gentiles also? (Romans 3:29)

But the belief in Israel's election is not just a theological issue, it has had political fallout as well. Some people, Jew and Christian, justify the existence of the modern State of Israel as the fulfillment of God's promise to Abraham that his descendants would possess the land forever (Genesis 13:15, 18–19; 17:8). They reject attempts at trading land for peace and oppose the establishment of a Palestinian state as contrary to the will of God as expressed in Scripture. This perspective is especially strong among some Evangelical Christians. Because of the political influence these Christians have in the United States, their beliefs about Israel as the chosen people have the potential of influencing American foreign policy and of postponing a political agreement between the State of Israel and the Palestinian

Authority. On a trip to Israel in October 2004, American tel-evangelist Pat Robertson asserted that the establishment of a Palestinian state would threaten Israel's existence and inter-fere with "God's plan."

Clearly the notion that Israel is God's chosen people has raised serious theological and political issues. What does the Bible itself say about this belief? How can Christians today appreciate and celebrate God's choice of Abraham and his descendants? What does this belief say about God's relation-ship with gentiles? As Saint Paul asked, "…is God the God of Jews only?" Paul posed this question rhetorically. He was con-vinced that the Christians of Rome to whom he wrote would answer a resounding "no" (see Romans 3:29). Still, a careful reading of Paul's letter to the Romans makes it clear that the answer to Paul's question is only deceptively simple. It is to this question that we now turn.

God's Choice

The term that expresses the idea of God's choice of Israel as God's people in a unique way is *election*. This word attempts to capture the perspective found in Deuteronomy 7:6b: "…the LORD your God has chosen you [Israel] out of all the peoples on earth to be his people, his treasured possession." Implicit in the choice of one alternative is the rejection of all others. That is the problem that most people have with the notion of election and is precisely what Paul had in mind when he posed his rhetorical question: "…is God the God of Jews only?" (Romans 3:29). There is, however, only one Old Testament text that actually says that God chose Israel and rejected another nation:

> I have loved you, says the LORD. But you say, "How have
> you loved us?" Is not Esau Jacob's brother? says the LORD.
> Yet I have loved Jacob but I have hated Esau.... (Malachi
> 1:2–3)

This text reflects the frustration experienced by the people
of Judah when their hopes for a glorious restoration following the return from exile in Babylon did not materialize.
The prophet lashes out at Edomites, Judah's southeastern
neighbors who were thought of as descendants of Esau,
Jacob's (Israel's) estranged brother (see Genesis 36:1). The
Edomites took advantage of Judah's weakness by snatching a
large swath of Judahite territory south of Jerusalem. But the
people of Judah faced a problem far more serious than the
loss of some territory. The tragic exile and the disappointing
restoration challenged Judah's core religious beliefs. How
can the Jews claim to know the God who created the universe
when no other nation does? Why were they the sole benefi-
ciary of God's revelation? What was the purpose of God's
choice of Abraham and his descendants?

The Jews believed in the one God who is the source of all
that is, but who chose one people as God's own:

> Although heaven and the heaven of heavens belong to the
> LORD your God, the earth with all that is in it, yet the LORD
> set his heart in love on your ancestors alone and chose
> you, their descendants after them, out of all the peo-
> ples...". (Deuteronomy 10:14–15)

This remarkable text describes God as having fallen in love
with Israel's forebears. The consequence was Israel's election. The significance of that election becomes clear in the

stories of Abraham and of the deliverance of his descendants from slavery in Egypt.

The story of Abraham does depict God singling out one person and his family for a special destiny (Genesis 12:1–3). God promises to bless Abraham in order to equip him for the fulfillment of his destiny (verse 2). That destiny is nothing less than the fulfillment of God's intention to extend the blessing of Abraham to "all the families of the earth" (verse 3). Israel's election, then, has a universal purpose. The story of Abraham, however, does not describe how Israel is to fulfill its destiny. The New Testament sees Jesus of Nazareth as the fulfillment of that destiny. But religious and even secular Jews today still wrestle with how they can live their lives so as to be a blessing to the nations. Some hold that the State of Israel has a unique responsibility to be "a light to the nations" (Isaiah 42:6; 49:6), especially by embodying the divine justice that calls for special concern for "the orphan, widow and alien" (see Deuteronomy 10:17–18). One tragedy of the Arab-Israeli conflict is that concern for the security of Israel's citizens makes it difficult for the State of Israel to fulfill that destiny. Those preoccupied with their own safety do not readily see the challenges others face.

Election and Justice

The Exodus of the Hebrew slaves from Egypt exemplifies the association between election and God's concern for justice:

> "I have observed the misery of my people who are in Egypt.…Indeed, I know their sufferings, and I have come down to deliver them.… (Exodus 3:7–8)

God is determined to end the exploitation of the Hebrew slaves. They will no longer serve at the whim of the pharaoh but will be free to seek their own happiness and prosperity in the land to which God will bring them. But the biblical text reinforces that this act of deliverance was the result of God's love for Israel's ancestors rather than a response to Israel's own worth:

> It was not because you were more numerous than any other people that the LORD set his heart on you and chose you—for you were the fewest of all peoples. It was because the LORD loved you and kept the oath that [the Lord] swore to your ancestors.... (Deuteronomy 7:7–8)

Again, the motivation for Israel's election is God's love of this people. This love expresses itself in concrete form when God led Abraham's descendants from slavery in Egypt to freedom in the land God promised to their ancestors.

The land that God promised Abraham was not empty. The connection between God's justice and God's love for Israel was as difficult for Judah's theologians to see as it is for readers today. The stories of the conquest in the book of Joshua appear to belie God's justice and love. These theologians make it clear that Israel was able to dispossess the Canaanites because of their wickedness. Still, Israel was not to conclude that the victories over the Canaanites were due to Israel's virtue. Moses cautions the people of Israel as they are about cross the Jordan and enter Canaan:

> When the LORD your God thrusts them [the people of Canaan] out before you, do not say to yourself, "It is because of my righteousness that the LORD has brought me in to occupy this land"; it is rather because of the wickedness of these nations that the LORD is dispossessing them before you. (Deuteronomy 9:4)

The results of archaeological investigation interpreted with anthropological and sociological categories suggest that the stories of Israel's conquest of Canaan was not simply a matter of an invading force of Israelites being challenged by the Canaanites who were reacting to the intrusion of a foreign group into the land. It is probable that most of the first Israelites were people on the bottom of the Canaanite social and economic ladder. They withdrew their loyalty from an unjust and oppressive social system and pledged it to the God of Israel, a nonhuman Lord who defends the poor against exploitation by the rich and powerful. These poor peasants became the nucleus of the Israelite tribes. Here is one example of archaeology undercutting the historical nature of the biblical story, but upholding the religious values implicit in the biblical tradition as a whole. Israel's acquisition of its land also shows the connection between God's love and justice.

Israel's Response

Israel, however, is not to be a passive recipient of God's love. It is to respond with love and fidelity. Election, then, is bound up with covenant:

> You have seen what I did to the Egyptians, and how I bore you on eagles' wings and brought you to myself. Now therefore, if you obey my voice and keep my covenant, you shall be my treasured possession out of all the peoples. (Exodus 19:4–5)

Ancient Israel's theologians used the term "covenant" as a metaphor to speak of Israel's relationship with God. "Covenant" is a term borrowed from the sphere of international relations. Perhaps the closest modern parallel is a treaty, which regulates some aspect of the relations between two or more nations. Some of ancient Israel's theologians found the term "covenant" a convenient way to describe Israel's responsibility toward God. Like a small nation that enjoys the protection of a great power, so Israel enjoys God's beneficent care. In return, Israel owes God commitment, obedience and loyalty. As God's elect, then, Israel has the obligation to obey the divine will as revealed in the commandments and laws that are part of the covenant-making process (see Exodus 20—23). It is little wonder that when the book of Deuteronomy mentions Israel's election, it immediately cautions Israel to obey God's commandments (see Deuteronomy 7:6–11; 10:12–20; 14:1–2; 28:1). While Israel's election is a gift from God, it carries with it grave responsibilities.

The Prophets on Election
The story of Israel in its land (Joshua—2 Kings) is a sad and tragic story. It is a story of Israel's disloyalty and disobedience. The prophet Amos speaks about the consequences of Israel's disloyalty:

> You only have I known
>   of all the families of the earth;
> therefore I will punish you
>   for all your iniquities.
> (Amos 3:2)

Israel's unique relationship with God ought to have been all the motivation it needed to create and maintain a society in which justice guided people's lives. Instead, Amos witnessed the corruption and venality of Israel's leadership and the neglect and even oppression of the poor. Other nations could assert their ignorance of God's demands, but Israel could not. Its election brought with it responsibilities that Israel could ignore only at its peril. Amos proclaims that Israel will have to face the most severe consequences for its infidelity precisely because of its election.

Some Israelites no doubt thought of election as a guarantee of God's favor, believing that to preserve God's own honor, God had to protect Israel from every threat to its existence. Amos and other prophets who preached about the same time sought to dislodge such a false assumption from Israel's beliefs. They did this in different ways—usually by announcing the inevitability of divine judgment. Most often Christians envision ancient Israel's prophets as calling for repentance. Indeed, occasionally some did call upon Israel to repent (see Jeremiah 26:13; Ezekiel 14:6). Most, however, did not, but instead announced the judgment that was coming upon Israel for its infidelity. There were some prophets who proclaimed their message through symbolic actions. Isaiah, for example, gave his son the improbable name *Maher-shalal-hash-baz* (Isaiah 8:3), which is Hebrew for "the spoil speeds, the prey hastens." The prophet was convinced that Israel was rushing toward a judgment that would be its undoing because it was oblivious to the consequences of its infidelity (see Isaiah 6:9–10).

Speaking more to Israel's reliance on its election to escape judgment, God ordered Hosea to name his son *Lo-ammi* [Not my people] (Hosea 1:8). Israel's election was, in fact, no guarantee. Its infidelity and disobedience led to a break-down of the relationship between God and Israel. The identity of Israel as God's chosen was no more for they were *Lo-ammi*. Still, the book of Hosea affirms that judgment is not God's last word to Israel and asserts "…in the place where it was said to [Israel], 'You are not my people,' it shall be said to them, 'Children of the living God'" (Hosea 1:10). Hosea's son will be renamed *Ammi* [My people] (Hosea 2:3; 2:1, ET). Israel will have to face the consequences of its infidelity but that infidelity does not nullify God's choice and commitment. Israel will once again be God's chosen.

The Election of the Nations

The prophet Isaiah takes the notion of Israel's election to a new level in 19:19–25. He envisions the building of an altar to Yahweh in the center of Egypt. Assyria too will join Egypt in the worship of Israel's God. God will call Egypt "my people" and Assyria "the work of my hands." It is difficult to overstate the significance of these images when one remembers that Israel was trapped as in a vise between Egypt to the south and Assyria to the north. It could not escape being drawn into the conflicts between these great powers. Isaiah implies that the ultimate purpose of Israel's election was the inclusion of all the world's nations among the People of God. The distinction between Israel and the nations, then, is only temporary and provisional. Second Isaiah takes up this very idea some two hundred years later and affirms that the nations will accept God's offer of salvation and will become "the offspring of Israel" (see Isaiah 45:20–25). This transformation does not mean that the prophet envisions Israel as a political power in a position of dominance over the nations;

rather, the prophet sees the nations joining Israel in the worship of Yahweh. The nations that were apparently passed over by God when God chose Israel will one day be included among the People of God, and so Israel's election reaches its destiny: "...in you all the families of the earth shall be blessed" (Genesis 12:3).

The Isaianic tradition continued to play with the idea of election. The last portions of that tradition to be written (chapters 56—66) see the basis of election in a peoples' moral character rather than in their national origins. Isaiah 65, for example, makes no division between Israel and the nations; rather, it sees God's chosen as those who are faithful (verses 9, 15, 22) as opposed to the rebellious (verses 1–7). If Israel's past has taught it anything, it should be that simple physical descent from Abraham means nothing. Israel—indeed all nations—will have a blessed future if they live as God's servants (65:8, 9, 13–15). At the same time, political, social and economic developments in the life of the Jewish community in and around Jerusalem led the Jewish community to turn in on itself. Following the return from exile, emphasis on practices such as circumcision, Sabbath observance and dietary laws became very strong. Such practices provided the Jewish community with a distinct religious identity. These practices coupled with the insistence that Jews marry within their community (Ezra 10; Nehemiah 10, 13) tended to blunt the universalist thrust of the Isaianic tradition. The book of Ezra in decrying marriages outside the community speaks of "the holy seed" (9:2), which has to be kept from being polluted by contact with the nations. The Jewish community of the fifth and fourth centuries had to deal with the very real prospect of extinction. The emphasis on maintaining a strong Jewish identity prevented the Jews from simply disappearing into the pages of history as did many ancient Near Eastern peoples. This development effectively blunted the notion that the election of Israel will reach its final destiny in the election of all nations.

The emphasis on the moral criterion for election refocused the idea of election from that of the entire people of Israel to individual election for members of the remnant, that is, what remains of the community that has been subject to God's judgment. The election of individuals became an especially important motif in some of the Dead Sea Scrolls. The community that produced those scrolls arose in response to the serious dispute among Jews of the second century B.C. over the priesthood and the temple. The people on the losing side of this dispute retired to a settlement near the Dead Sea and awaited God's final intervention in Israel's life, when they fully expected to be vindicated. They believed that God had chosen specific individuals to be part of their community, saving them from inclusion with "false" Israel. Individuals were predestined to join the community at the Dead Sea, and when made aware of their calling, they would be sure to separate themselves from "false" Israel and join the community at the Dead Sea.

Paul on Election

In recounting Paul's success with evangelizing the people of Antioch in Pisidia, the Acts of the Apostles comments, "...as many as had been destined for eternal life became believers" (13:48). This assertion of individual election is quite similar to the ideology of the community at the Dead Sea, but Acts is recounting Paul's success among the gentiles after being rebuffed by the Jewish community of Antioch (see Acts 13:14–48, especially verses 44–48). In appropriating the notion of election from early Judaism, the first Christians tended to focus on the election of individuals. This is especially obvious in the writing of Saint Paul. Reflecting on his own experience, Paul concluded that his transformation from one who persecuted those who followed the way of Jesus Christ to one who devoted his entire energy to the proclamation of the gospel must be due to God's choice—not his own:

> You have heard…of my earlier life in Judaism. I was violently persecuting the church of God…. But when God, who has set me apart before I was born…was pleased to reveal his Son to me, so that I might proclaim him among the Gentiles…. (Galatians 1:13–16)

Paul uses this understanding of election to deal with what was for him a great personal and theological problem: the failure of the mission to the Jews, which he discusses at length in Romans 9—11. He asserted that the reason few Jews have come to believe in the gospel is that God has not elected all Jews to believe in Jesus (see Romans 9:6–15). Paul believed that God's choice in this matter was prior to the existence of the individuals who had to choose for or against Christ. At the same time, Paul held to the election of Israel, but he redefined Israel as the sum of elect Jews (that is, those who believe in Christ) and the elect gentiles (that is, those who share in the blessings of Abraham).

A significant difference between election as described in the Old Testament and Paul's understanding of this notion is that the apostle focuses his attention on God as the chooser of the elect, rather than on the beneficiaries of that choice:

> ...God chose you as the first fruits for salvation through sanctification by the Spirit and through belief in the truth.
> (2 Thessalonians 2:13b)

The fourth Gospel mirrors Paul's refocusing of the election motif, but this Gospel makes Jesus the chooser—along with God—of the elect:

> You did not choose me but I chose you. And appointed you to go and bear fruit.... (John 15:16)

Notice the Deuteronomic-like connection between election and the "bearing fruit." The beneficiaries of God's choice cannot remain passive recipients of God's blessing. Like Abraham they are to become agents of the blessing that they have received.

Election in the Church's Tradition

When Christian theologians have reflected on the election motif, they have followed Paul's lead and have focused on God who exercises divine sovereignty in the act of election. Augustine taught that some people were chosen for salvation while others for damnation. Election was the result of God's will and God's grace. The Reformers, following Augustine, believed that God's choice of individuals was the first step in their salvation. Their election was due to neither their good works nor their faith. It was a pure act of grace—an exercise of divine sovereignty. The Roman Catholic position is closer to that of Deuteronomy, because it emphasizes the connection between election and obedience. While election is an unmerited act of divine grace, the elect are called to respond to that grace with love, fidelity and commitment. They are called to "bear fruit" and bear it abundantly.

Though some see "election" as an emphasis in Protestant theology, the Roman Catholic liturgy uses the language of election frequently. Here are just two examples. First, in the Roman Canon (Eucharistic Prayer I), the presider prays just before the words of institution: "Father, accept this offering from your whole family. Grant us your peace in this life, save us from final damnation, and count us among those you have chosen."

Second, one component of the Rite of Christian Initiation of Adults is the "Rite of Election." This normally takes place on the first Sunday of Lent at the cathedral with the bishop as presider. First, the sponsors testify that the catechumens are ready to continue their preparation to receive the sacraments of initiation. The bishop then welcomes the catechumens as "the elect of God" and asks them to sign "the Book of the Elect." The individuals preparing themselves to receive the sacraments of initiation during the Easter Vigil enter the cathedral as catechumens but leave as "the elect."

The use of the election language of the Bible is a way that the liturgy acknowledges the church's unique relationship with Judaism. We are claiming a connection with the family of Abraham whom God has chosen to be a blessing to all nations. Appropriating this language involves an obvious reinterpretation of the biblical idea. The elect are not only the physical descendants of Abraham, but people from every nation who have been "grafted in" to the community of believers that God has chosen. By the grace of God, we, like "wild olive shoots," have been grafted into the olive tree that is the community of the elect (see Romans 11:17–24).

The liturgy uses election language to make it clear that we are who we are by the grace of God. When we reflect on our election, we need to recall the words of Deuteronomy, which reminded the ancient Israelites that their election was not due to any unique qualities or achievements on their part. The election of Israel can be explained only by God's love. It only remains for the elect to respond enthusiastically to that love (see Deuteronomy 7:7–11).

The Election of the Poor

Another example of the appropriation of the election motif by Christians is provided by liberation theologians. For them the "elect" are the poor and oppressed whom God chooses over the rich and powerful. This, of course, derives from the story of the Exodus in which God chooses the oppressed Hebrew slaves and delivers them from the power of the pharaoh. According to these theologians, the God of the Bible is known by God's determination to free the oppressed. Election is inseparable from the establishment of God's justice for the poor. Clearly the biblical stories that have election as an important motif deal with people on the margins of society. Abraham was a stranger in the land of Canaan, moving there from his home in Mesopotamia by a divine impulse. Deuteronomy speaks of Jacob and a "wandering Aramean" who went down to Egypt driven by hunger.

Jacob's descendants were enslaved there only to be freed by the power of God and brought to a land that made freedom and prosperity possible (see Deuteronomy 26:5–10).

To speak about election in today's context, marked as it is by the great disparity between rich and poor, is to speak about God's "preferential option for the poor," to use a phrase popularized by liberation theologians. The practical consequence of God's choice of the poor is the necessity of asking "How will this affect the poor?" and "Does this promote justice?" whenever embarking on a course of action. The United States is a very wealthy country with a majority of its citizens living comfortably. In such a situation, it becomes easy to ignore the poor, who are treated as insignificant politically, economically and socially. At most, the poor are nameless statistics in government reports. It is a challenge to remember the poor. At this point, the church makes its great contribution to society. The community of faith is composed of people who are "the elect," chosen because of God's preferential option for those in need. The obvious response of "the elect" is to act the same way toward the poor, that is, those most in need in our society. The biblical motif of election is a way of speaking about "divine partiality." What liberation theologians are saying is that this "divine partiality" must find expression in the life of the church. For the church to be obedient to the divine will it must make a "preferential option for the poor."

There are members of the community of faith who find it necessary to distinguish themselves from those outside the community. Following their return from exile, the Jews felt that need. They began to emphasize practices such as Sabbath observance, the dietary laws, circumcision and marriages within the community as means of self-definition. How will the Christian "elect" distinguish themselves? Some may suggest that the church's theological doctrines provide believers with an identity. There is a strong push for doctrinal orthodoxy that is moving in the direction of doctrinal uniformity, and respect for theological pluralism is labeled "dissent." Others suggest ritual separation as the dividing line that clearly identifies the "elect." But the biblical motif of election makes it clear that the church's moral practice should be the way the community distinguishes itself. In today's context, a moral imperative is the "preferential option for the poor."

Catholics find the Bible's motif of election to be somewhat problematic. Does God actually show partiality to one people, one group, one class over others? The biblical tradition is founded on the belief that God did choose the descendants of Abraham. But God's election of that family was to insure that "all the families of the earth" be blessed (see Genesis 12:3). God did choose some to come to faith in Jesus Christ, and the apostle affirms, "…it depends not on human will or exertion, but on God who shows mercy" (Romans 9:16). So the church prays, "…count us among those you have chosen" (the Roman Canon). Some may find the notion of election and the sovereign freedom of God a type of Jewish and Christian fatalism. The value of this biblical motif for believers depends upon the church's creativity in translating "election" from an idea into an engine moving its life. This will not be a simple matter for many Christians since "election" will challenge not only their religious ideas but especially their ways of living. Christians can indeed celebrate their election, but they can never be content with merely being passive recipients of God's choice. Like Abraham, all believers were chosen to be instruments and agents of blessing. In today's context, this means making the preferential option for the poor. God has chosen the poor to be God's special possession; those who live by the ideals of the gospel cannot do otherwise.

QUESTIONS FOR REFLECTION

1. Why did God choose Israel to be a people particularly God's own?
2. What responsibilities flowed from Israel's election?
3. What is the relationship between election and justice?
4. What did the prophets say about Israel's election?
5. In what ways does Paul's notion of election differ from that in the Old Testament?
6. How does the church use the language of election?
7. How does the "preferential option for the poor" relate to the motif of election?

FOR FURTHER READING

Bowman, Donna. *The Divine Decision: A Process Doctrine of Election*. Louisville: Westminster John Knox, 2002.

DeFraine, Jean. *The Bible on Vocation and Election*. De Pere, Wis.: St. Norbert Abbey Press, 1966.

Gutíerrez, Gustavo. *A Theology of Liberation*. Maryknoll, N.Y.: Orbis, 1973.

Hoppe, Leslie J. *There Shall Be No Poor Among You: Poverty in the Bible*. Nashville: Abingdon, 2004.

Lohfink, Norbert. *Option for the Poor: The Basic Principle of Liberation Theology in Light of the Bible.* Berkeley, Calif.: BIBAL, 1987.

Rowley, Harold H. *The Biblical Doctrine of Election.* London: Lutterworth, 1950.

CHAPTER FIVE

How Does God Speak?

Christians believe the Bible to be "the Word of God." Now there are about four hundred references to the Word of God in the Old Testament. The expression that appears most frequently is "the word of the Lord," occurring 240 times. Most often this phrase refers to a word "from" God. The Bible then assumes that God communicates with human beings in an intelligible way so that the divine can be known and fulfilled by human beings. The people of ancient Israel believed in a God who could and did speak to them, who did reveal the divine will, who spoke at precise times and for specific purposes. But how precisely does this process work? Does God "speak" directly to human beings? Is there some technique or ritual that is necessary to facilitate communication between God and God's human creatures?

There are two ways to answer these questions. One is to focus on ancient Israel's popular religion, and the other is to look at its "official" religion. The Bible, as an expression of Israel's "official religion," offers insights into popular religion as it criticizes various rituals and practices. For example, Elijah condemns the penchant that his fellow Israelites had for serving both the Lord and Baal (1 Kings 18:21). Ezekiel witnesses women engaged in the ritual weeping for the god Tammuz in the Jerusalem temple (Ezekiel 8:14). Deuteronomy condemns divination or the use of omens to determine the divine will (18:9–14).

Divination

Divination is based on the belief that messages from the gods lie hidden in omens and that someone especially skilled is needed—someone who understands the significance of omens and so is able to decipher those messages. The Deuteronomic legislation itself is a testimony to the popularity of divinatory practices in ancient Israel. This popularity is confirmed by archaeology, which has uncovered artifacts such as clay liver models used by diviners to catalog the significance of abnormalities on the livers of sacrificed animals. It was assumed that the gods used these abnormalities as a way to communicate with people.

Divination was a significant part of religious practice in Mesopotamia for more than a millennium before the Israelite tribes emerged in Canaan. There were two types of omens that were significant for the process of divination. The first were naturally occurring phenomena—especially deviations from the normal such as defective births, changes in the appearance of the nighttime sky, unusual cloud formations and dreams. A second type of omen included those induced by the diviner such as the patterns made by dropping oil on water, or by the smoke from incense, or by special sticks thrown by the diviner, or by the casting of lots. People believed that the gods used these phenomena to communicate with human beings. For example, Ezekiel 21:21 describes the king of Babylon using three divinatory methods (the shaking of arrows, the consultation of *teraphim* [images of the gods] and the examination of an animal's liver) to determine which way to turn at a crossroad.

The problem is that the messages were ambiguous and easily misunderstood, requiring specially trained and skilled interpreters to decipher communication from the gods. The purpose of divination was not simply to know the divine will but, more important, to help people take appropriate measures to avoid any evil that was foreseen by the diviner. For example, if a person wished to know if a particular illness would lead to death, and the diviner, after consulting the omens, affirmed that it would, the person who asked for the consultation would not simply accept the will of the gods and prepare for death. That person would engage in some ritual activity—wearing an amulet, saying a prayer, making an offering to a shrine or going on a pilgrimage—that would serve to "change" the god's mind, and the evil would be averted.

When Deuteronomy forbids the practice of divination, it does not suggest that omen-seeking does not work. The assumption is that it does. But such practices are forbidden to Israel because they involve attempts to manipulate the divine will, as if God could be controlled by some sort of ritual activity.

Deuteronomy affirms that the only way Israel could assure its future was through obedience to the written authoritative Torah—not by attempting to manipulate God by wearing an amulet, for example. But the lure of divination is too strong to be eliminated by a simple command. In fact, some forms of divination enjoy approval in the Bible. For example, the Old Testament considers the casting of lots to be an acceptable form of divination. Exodus 28:30 speaks of two objects that the priest carried with himself: the *urim* and *thummim*. Apparently these were two objects that enabled the priest to choose between two alternatives in a time of crisis—personal or national. First Samuel 14:41–42 illustrates the use of these lot oracles to determine who was responsible for God's disfavor on Saul and his army. The first Christian community also used the lot oracle, believing as their ancestors did that God controlled how lots fell. They chose Matthias to take Judas's place by lot (Acts 1:26).

Another form of divination that the Old Testament considered legitimate was the interpretation of dreams. Jacob's favorite son Joseph proved to be a very accurate interpreter of dreams. At times his skill got him into trouble (Genesis 37:9–11) while at other times it saved him. Joseph's ability to interpret the dream of the pharaoh led to his elevation as the pharaoh's vizier (Genesis 41:1–57). Similarly, Daniel's ability to both tell and interpret Nebuchadnezzar's dream led to his promotion in the king's court in Babylon (Daniel 2). Solomon's dream at Gibeon confirmed him as David's successor with a gift of wisdom to rule (1 Kings 3). Again, the New Testament also shows confidence in dreams as a means of divine-human communication. It was through dreams that Joseph received instructions to wed Mary (Matthew 1:20), to take Mary and Jesus to Egypt (Matthew 2:13), and then to settle with them in Nazareth (Matthew 2:19).

The Prophetic Word

The most characteristic form of divine-human communication in ancient Israel was through prophecy. In the mind of many Israelites, prophets were associated with foretelling the future. For example, when Saul searched for his father's lost livestock, he consulted a "prophet" for help in finding them (1 Samuel 9:9). When Jehoshaphat of Judah and Ahab of Israel considered going to war with the king of Aram, they first consulted four hundred prophets who predicted victory (1 Kings 22:6) and then, at Jehoshaphat's insistence, they consulted one more who predicted defeat (1 Kings 22:17). An infallible sign of God's rejection of Saul was God's refusal to make the divine will known to Saul on the eve of a battle with the Philistines either through a dream, the *urim* and *thummim*, or through a prophet (1 Samuel 28:6).

Most Christians associate prophets with the call to repentance—primarily because of the way the liturgy uses readings from the prophetic books.

The prophetic books, however, present the prophets as those entrusted by God to deliver a message to Israel. That message took two basic forms. The prophets first announced the consequences of the choices that Israel made. Israel chose not to maintain a society based on justice. People of means corrupted the judicial system in order to increase their holdings at the expense of the Israelite peasant. Priests presided over a liturgy that dulled people's sensitivity to the injustices of the Israelite social and economic system. Instead of insuring that the peasants' rights were protected, Israelite kings facilitated the growth of social inequity. In addition to social injustice, both Israelite kingdoms were guilty of compromising their ancestral religious traditions by failing to serve the Lord alone. The worship of foreign deities became all the rage and took place even within the confines of the temple itself (see Ezekiel 8:14–15). Prophets such as Amos, Hosea, Micah, Isaiah, Jeremiah and Ezekiel announced God's judgment on Israel's behavior. That judgment would be nothing less than the destruction of Israel's political and economic system at the hands of foreign invaders, the loss of the land and the exile of the people. Israel's religious institutions were not exempt from judgment. The Jerusalem temple was to be destroyed and its priesthood scattered (see Micah 3:9–12).

Some prophets, however, proclaimed that they had received a different message from the Lord. Jeremiah 28 preserves an encounter between Jeremiah and a prophet named Hananiah. Jeremiah had been walking about Jerusalem with a yoke around his neck (see Jeremiah 27:1—28:17) to dramatize his belief that Babylon's subjugation of Judah was at God's command and that any attempt at rebellion would be against the divine will. Hananiah announced that Babylon's domination of Judah was about to end (Jeremiah 28:1–5), and to dramatize this word from God, Hananiah took the yoke from Jeremiah's shoulder and broke it (Jeremiah 28:10). Hananiah believed that the conflict between Judah and Babylon was determined by a conflict going on in the heavens between the Lord, Judah's patron deity, and

Marduk, the god of Babylon. Of course, there could be only one outcome of such a conflict—the Lord would be victorious so Judah could count on a military and political victory over Babylon.

Jeremiah believed that the outcome of conflict between Judah and Babylon was determined by a conflict within Judah itself—the conflict between the powerful and the powerless. The people of means, the royal and judicial establishment, and even the priesthood were arrayed against the poor. Judah's social, political and economic systems were geared for the benefit of the wealthy at the expense of the peasants. Jeremiah believed that in a conflict between the powerful and the powerless, the Lord always takes the side of the poor (see Job 34:28; Deuteronomy 24:15). Jeremiah believed that God was using Babylon to execute judgment on Judah because of the oppression of its poor by people of means. He asserted that God had not sent Hananiah and his pronouncements were not to be trusted (Jeremiah 28:15). Jeremiah then wrote a letter to the exiles advising them to prepare themselves for a long stay in Babylon (see Jeremiah 29).

When the two kingdoms ceased to exist and their territory was annexed by the Mesopotamian empires, when the last of the Israelite kings were deposed, when Jerusalem's temple was destroyed, and when the people and their leaders were led into exile, people remembered the words of the prophets like Jeremiah. They concluded that the fall of their national states was not due to the military and political power of Assyria and Babylon but was the working out of the divine will. The kingdoms of Israel and Judah reaped the whirlwind sown by the injustice that was endemic to the two Israelite national states. But there was a second aspect to the prophets' message. While they spoke about the inevitability of divine judgment, they were convinced that judgment was not God's final word to Israel. The prophets believed in Israel's ultimate restoration. In addition to announcing Israel's judgment, they proclaimed its salvation. This is nowhere more movingly expressed than in the words of an anonymous prophet whose words have been associated with those of Isaiah:

> Comfort, O comfort my people,
>   says your God.
> Speak tenderly to Jerusalem,
>   and cry to her
> that she has served her term,
>   that her penalty is paid,
> that she has received from the LORD's hand
>   double for all her sins.
> (Isaiah 40:1–2)

These touching words suggest that God was excessive in judgment ("double for all her sins"). Ancient Israel's prophets did look to the future—but it was a future in which God would free Israel from the consequences of its folly—a future in which justice and peace would reign—a future in which Israel would be guided by "a new heart" and "a new spirit" (see Ezekiel 8:26). Israel's relationship with God would be cemented by a "new covenant" (see Jeremiah 31:31–32). The Christian church believes that these prophetic visions were fulfilled in Jesus Christ, who described the contents of the cup he shared with his friends on the night before he died as his blood sealing the "new covenant" (see Luke 22:20).

Though ancient Israel's prophets have always been associated with the "word of God," they were not the only way that God chose to communicate with Israel:

> ...for instruction shall not perish from the priest, nor counsel from the wise, nor the word from the prophet. (Jeremiah 18:18)

The Torah of the Priests

The Hebrew word, which the *New Revised Standard Version Bible* translates as "instruction" in the above citation from Jeremiah 18 is *torah*. This word originally referred to the answers priests gave to questions posed to them regarding areas in which they were the acknowledged experts. For example, if people had questions about the kinds of animals acceptable for sacrifice, the foods that were proper to eat, matters of purity and impurity, they asked the priests. Eventually, these answers to specific questions were assembled into collections. Certain biblical texts (for example, Leviticus 1—7; 11; 13—14; 25; Exodus 25—31; 35—40) likely represent such collections. These texts may have even served as a reference work to be consulted by priests serving in the temple as they were undergoing training for their service.

Though ancient Israel's priests were responsible for the worship of the Lord, they were not simply liturgical ministers; they had other responsibilities. The blessing of Moses on the tribe of Levi from which ancient Israel's priests came specifies as one of these responsibilities teaching Israel God's laws (see Deuteronomy 33:8–11). The prophets criticized the priests severely for their failure to fulfill this responsibility:

> My people are destroyed for lack of knowledge;
>> because you have rejected knowledge,
> I reject you from being a priest to me.
> And since you have forgotten the law [torah] of your God,
>> I also will forget your children.
> (Hosea 4:6; see also 5:1; 6:9)

Israel's kings recognized the critical position that the priests played in society, so they attempted to co-opt them, making them royal officials. Instead of teaching people the need for maintaining a society based on justice, the priests were sometimes staunch defenders of the royal establishment. For example, when Amos came to Bethel and began speaking about the abuse of the poor at the hands of the wealthy—abuse abetted by the king—it was the priest Amaziah who expelled the prophet from the temple, explaining "…it is the king's sanctuary, and it is a temple of the kingdom" (Amos 7:13, see verses 10–17). Though Jeremiah belonged to a priestly family (Jeremiah 1:1), he singled out priests for special condemnation very often in his oracles (see 1:18; 2:8, 26; 4:9; 5:31; 6:13; 8:1, 10; 13:13; 14:18; 23:11, 33—34; 32:32; 34:19). In his view, priests were not fulfilling their responsibility to teach Israel torah.

Following the return of the Jews from exile in Babylon, priests played a key role in the reconstitution of Jewish life in Jerusalem. First, it is likely that priests assembled ancient

Israel's narrative and legal traditions into what we now know as the Pentateuch (the five books of Moses). In Hebrew, these five books are known as Torah, the word for "priestly instruction." It was a priest named Ezra who promulgated the Torah and called for the assent of the people to shape their lives according to the sacred text (Nehemiah 8; see Ezra 7:12).

A dominant metaphor used in the letter to the Hebrews to explain the person and work of Jesus Christ is the ancient Israelite priesthood. Jesus is the "high priest" according to the order of Melchizedek (Hebrews 6:20) who offered one sacrifice for all (Hebrews 5:10; 9:11, 25). The book of Hebrews, then, understands the priesthood of Jesus as unique (Hebrews 7:12, 24). But citing Exodus 2:9, 1 Peter 2:9 asserts that God has formed the newly baptized into a "royal priesthood." The *Catechism of the Catholic Church* has recognized this as "the common priesthood of all believers" (#1268). The New Testament does not offer an example of someone called a priest presiding at the Eucharist. The church's ministerial priesthood is based on the model found in the Old Testament as the prayer of consecration in the ritual of priestly ordination said by the ordaining bishop makes clear:

> When you had appointed high priests to rule your people, you chose other men next to them in rank and dignity to be with them and to help them in their task; and so there grew up the ranks of priests and the offices of Levites, established by sacred rites....You shared among the sons of Aaron the fullness of their father's power, to provide

worthy priests in sufficient number for the increasing rites of sacrifice and worship. With the same loving care, you gave companions to your Son's apostles to help in teaching the faith: they preached the gospel to the whole world.

Like their Old Testament counterparts, Catholic priests are responsible for more than fulfilling their liturgical functions. They too are to impart "priestly instruction," that is, they are to hand on the tradition that they have received, interpreting that tradition for and with the people of God.

The Guidance of the Elders

The elders of ancient Israel, like the priests, were responsible for handing on the norms of traditional Israelite morality to succeeding generations. They may not have been as formally constituted as were the priests, but they still had a very significant role to play in Israel's life. The elders exercised judicial functions in the community before the monarchy became an institution in Israel's life. They were the older, wiser and more experienced members of the village to whom their neighbors went to settle disputes, get advice and learn the traditions of their ancestors. The Bible portrays them as sitting at the city gate where they were of service to the community (see Deuteronomy 21:2, 19; 25:7; Ruth 4:1–2; Amos 5:10, 15). The elders were instrumental in the establishment of the monarchy. They asked Samuel to appoint a king for Israel (1 Samuel 8:4–5). David was able to persuade the elders of Judah to accept him as king (2 Samuel 2:1–4, 11). Seven years later the elders of Israel offered to accept David as king over the rest of the tribes (2 Samuel 5:1–5). One function of the elders was to remind the king that his authority was limited (see 2 Kings 12:6–7), but they could also be co-opted by monarchs who wished their authority over the subjects to be absolute (see 1 Kings 21:8–14). But it was a group of "elders of the land" who saved Jeremiah's life when he was accused of treason for announcing divine judgment on Jerusalem and its temple (see Jeremiah 26:17).

In administering justice according to the values of traditional Israelite morality, the elders insured the survival of these values. Indeed, these values form the basis of much of the legislation found in the Deuteronomic code (Deuteronomy 12—26). Most of the legislation found in Exodus, Leviticus and Numbers concerns matters especially significant to priests. Deuteronomy's legislation, on the other hand, focuses on issues related to family and civil life for the most part (see Deuteronomy 21:18–21; 22:13–21; 25:5–10). The elders were responsible for administering and transmitting these laws whose primary goal was insuring that the people of Israel could live an authentic community life. The Ten Commandments form a small compendium of the type of values that were transmitted by the elders. The commandments make community life possible. In order to sustain community life, people have to speak the truth to each other, respect each other's marital relationships and property. They need to care for their elderly parents. The content of the commandments, then, is not a matter of revelation. What is revelation—and what the elders teach—is that the creation and maintenance of a good community is the divine will for human beings and that access to God comes through the mediation of the community—that Israel's relationship with God is in some sense indirect, for it depends upon just relationships among the people of Israel. The New Testament makes similar affirmations:

> I give you a new commandment, that you love one another. Just as I have loved you, you also should love one another. By this everyone will know that you are my disciples, if you have love for one another. (John 13:34–35)

> Those who say, "I love God," and hate their brothers or sisters, are liars; for those who do not love a brother or sister whom they have seen, cannot love God whom they have not seen. (1 John 4:20)

The commandments describe the type of practical action that people must take to maintain an authentic community life. Again, the New Testament depicts Jesus as citing two texts from the Torah as summarizing Jewish moral tradition:

> (Jesus) said…: "'You shall love the Lord your God with all your heart, and with all your soul, and with all your mind.' This is the greatest and first commandment. And a second is like it: 'You shall love your neighbor as yourself.' On these two commandments hang all the law and the prophets." (Matthew 22:37–40)

The source for Jesus' "first commandment" is Deuteronomy 6:5, while Leviticus 19:18 is the source for the "second." The elders are the guardians and transmitters of this traditional morality of ancient Israel. More than anyone else, they are responsible for providing Judaism and Christianity with the ethical values that guide these two religious traditions. They have taught believers that just, loving, supportive human relationships are the barometers of the quality of any relationship with God.

The Wisdom of the Sages

In addition to the prophets, priests and elders, there is a fourth circle of ancient Israel's leadership that has transmitted the word of God to succeeding generations: Israel's sages, the "wise," who gave practical advice on how people can master life rather than be mastered by it. There are five books in the Old Testament canon used by Catholics that contain the teachings of the wise: Proverbs, Job, Ecclesiastes, Ecclesiasticus (Sirach) and Wisdom. The sages carefully observed peoples' actions in order to formulate general principles of conduct—which choices "work" and which do not. For example, they observed that pride, if not checked, will be a person's undoing:

> Pride goes before destruction,
>   and a haughty spirit before a fall.
> (Proverbs 16:18)

Unlike ancient Israel's other teachers, the wise did not maintain that their observations about life carried with them divine authority. The wise accepted responsibility for what they taught, recognizing the relativity of their own insights and suggesting that individuals carefully reflect on what they need to do in difficult situations. True wisdom is knowing what is the best choice to make when life presents us with several alternatives. For example, the sages provide two suggestions for dealing with fools:

> Do not answer fools according to their folly,
> or you will be a fool yourself.
> Answer fools according to their folly,
> or they will be wise in their own eyes.
> (Proverbs 26:4–5)

Seeing these two sayings next to each another leads the reader to think carefully about the implications of each. Sometimes it is necessary to treat fools as they deserve; other times it is better to avoid confrontation and embarrassment. It is necessary to assess each situation carefully before deciding which alternative to choose. Still, the sages recognize that no matter how deliberate in judgment one is, there is always one incalculable:

> The human mind plans the way,
> but the LORD directs the steps.
> (Proverbs 16:9)

God is beyond the reach of human planning and control, leading the sages to recognize the relativity of their insights. Still, they regard the search for wisdom and understanding as nothing less than a search for the divine, for wisdom was created "at the beginning of [God's] work, the first of [God's] acts" (Proverbs 8:22).

Qoheleth, the sage responsible for the book of Ecclesiastes, felt the inadequacy of the human mind in the search for wisdom most acutely. In his frustration, he suggested that God was responsible for making it impossible for human beings ever to acquire true wisdom:

> I have seen the business that God has given to everyone to
> be busy with. He has made everything suitable for its time;
> moreover he has put a sense of past and future into their
> minds, yet they cannot find out what God has done from
> the beginning to the end. (Ecclesiastes 3:10–11)

While Ecclesiastes was skeptical about the ability of human
beings to acquire wisdom, he did not allow that skepticism to
rob him of the simple joys of life:

> Go, eat your bread with enjoyment, and drink your wine
> with a merry heart; for God has long ago approved what
> you do. Let your garments always be white; do not let oil
> be lacking on your head. Enjoy life with the wife whom
> you love, all the days of your vain life that are given you
> under the sun, because that is your portion in life and in
> your toil at which you toil under the sun. Whatever your
> hand finds to do, do with your might; for there is no work
> or thought or knowledge or wisdom in Sheol, to which you
> are going. (Ecclesiastes 9:7–10)

The word *Sheol* as used by Ecclesiastes here refers to the
abode of the dead or the grave. The text asserts that people
need to grasp at whatever good comes their way before they
die because death brings an end to all human striving and
achievement. It is important to remember that the Semitic
peoples of the ancient Near East—Israel included—had no
expectation of life after death. It was the specter of death
that led Ecclesiastes to regard all efforts at attaining wisdom
futile. Since both the wise and the foolish die, what is the

point of working so hard to attain wisdom (see Ecclesiastes 2:12–26)? When precisely the notion of resurrection emerged in ancient Israel is not clear, but there are only two explicit references to it in the Hebrew Bible: Isaiah 26:19 and Daniel 12:2. Both these texts are late, coming from about the second century B.C. Some interpreters find in the poetry of the psalms indications that the belief in resurrection was much earlier. Still, even in Jesus' day, this belief was not universal among Jews (see Matthew 22:23; Mark 12:18; Luke 20:27).

Job admits that the idea of life beyond death would end the mental anguish that was the most serious component of the suffering he endured (see Job 14). But Job believed that any hope for a life after death that would bring vindication was pointless (verse 12). The suffering of Job was all the more grievous precisely because he could not expect a reversal of his fortunes in another world. That is precisely the reason he demanded that God explain things in the present (see Job 19). While Job agreed with his friends that God rewards the just and punishes the evil, Job insisted that he was an exception to this rule. Job's friends found such assertion astounding and did their best to convince him to admit his guilt and ask for God's mercy. In the end, Job did receive his vindication—not through a promise of eternal life but by having his family and fortune restored to him (Job 42:10–16).

Like the book of Ecclesiastes, Job too underscores the relativity of human insight into the divine. The book functions, in part, as a warning to Israel's sages not to put too much store in the wisdom they prize so highly and for which they work so diligently. Indeed, the sages can teach people how they might master life, but they must recognize that some circumstances may make their wisdom look like folly. Job is a case in point. His fortunes changed dramatically in an instant. He had no way to neutralize the power of evil that was taking control of his life. He did not understand what was happening to him. Eventually God would tell Job that he could not understand the evil that befell him—evil that he did not deserve (Job 38:1—42:6). Both Job and Ecclesiastes are evidence that ancient Israel's wise were aware of the limits of their wisdom.

Sirach, however, is fully confident that the sages' quest for wisdom can be successful—not because of human potential but because God commanded wisdom to find a home among the Jews:

> "Then the Creator of all things gave me a command,
>   and my Creator chose the place for my tent.
> He said, 'Make your dwelling in Jacob,
>   and in Israel receive your inheritance.'
> Before the ages, in the beginning, he created me,
>   and for all the ages I shall not cease to be.
> In the holy tent I ministered before him,
>   and so I was established in Zion.
> (Sirach 24:8–10)

For Sirach, acquiring wisdom is not some unattainable goal as both Ecclesiastes (2:18–23) and Job (28:1–27) thought. God made it possible for the Jews to find the way to wisdom—to the mastery of life—because God gave Israel the Torah. It is the Torah that leads to wisdom (Sirach 24:23).

Observance of Torah is not simply an act of obedience to a God who demands obedience from Israel; rather, Torah is the key to success, happiness and prosperity. It is the way to wisdom and all its rewards.

The book of Wisdom, also known as the Wisdom of Solomon, makes an assertion about the availability of wisdom similar to that made by Sirach. While Sirach has God direct wisdom to "make its dwelling in Jacob" (Sirach 24:8), the book of Wisdom shows the influence of Greek thought as it describes wisdom as an emanation of the Divine that pervades the entire world (Wisdom 7:22b—8:1). But the book also asserts that wisdom's perfect expression is found in God's revelation to Israel (see Wisdom 10:1–21). Wisdom is a unique book in the Roman Catholic canon of the Old Testament. It is the only Old Testament book to have been composed in Greek and, as such, is not part of the rabbinic canon. The rabbis accepted only books composed in Hebrew. It also has the distinction of being the last book of the Catholic Old Testament canon written, dating from about 50 B.C. It was composed in Alexandria to encourage Jews during a time of persecution. The author suggests that wisdom not only teaches people what pleases God, but is God's instrument though which the persecuted Jews will be saved (Wisdom 9:18). Acquiring wisdom, then, is not simply for the purpose of mastering life. Wisdom directs divine providence in saving the righteous in Israel and insuring that their persecutors receive the retribution they deserve.

Jesus: The Word of God
The New Testament speaks of Jesus as "the wisdom of God" (1 Corinthians 1:24). In speaking of the primacy of Christ,

1 Colossians 1:15–20 uses the language and thought of the hymns to wisdom found in the Old Testament (Proverbs 8; Sirach 24; Wisdom 6—9). Perhaps the most familiar and most thoroughgoing appropriation of wisdom thought and language is found in the prologue to John's Gospel (1:1–18). This passage calls Jesus "the Word" of God. But this Word is not merely speech. The Word is God's agent in this world and was with God in the beginning. The Old Testament makes similar affirmations about wisdom (see Proverbs 8:22–31; Wisdom 9:1).

This chapter began with a question that asked how God speaks to human beings. Christians believe that God speaks to us through ancient Israel's priests, prophets, elders and sages, and finally in a most definitive manner through the very Word of God—Jesus Christ. One of the early controversies in the Second Vatican Council concerned the sources of revelation. Some members of the Roman Curia insisted that there were two sources of revelation: Scripture and tradition. Speaking about revelation in this way sets Catholics apart from Protestant Christians, and some bishops and theologians were concerned about maintaining this distinction. Since John XXIII envisioned the Council as pastorally and ecumenically oriented, some of the bishops and theologians looked for a way to speak about revelation that both Catholic and Protestant Christians could accept. The Council's Dogmatic Constitution on Divine Revelation, *Dei Verbum*, begins with a clear articulation of just such a formula. Chapter one of that document affirms that the one source of revelation is Jesus Christ. The Word of God that is Jesus Christ reaffirms and perfects the word spoken through ancient Israel's priests, prophets, elders and sages. What remains for believers is to become not only hearers of the word but doers as well (see James 1:22).

QUESTIONS FOR REFLECTION

1. Where do you experience the Word of God touching your life?
2. What was the message of the prophets to the people of ancient Israel? Does that message speak to believers today?
3. How has the Old Testament priesthood helped shape the priesthood in the Catholic church today?
4. How did the elders contribute to the religious life of ancient Israel?
5. How did the sages' contribution to ancient Israel's religious thought differ from that of the priests, prophets and elders?

FOR FURTHER READING

Benoit, Pierre. *Aspects of Biblical Inspiration.* J. Murphy-O'Connor and S.K. Ashe, trans. Chicago: Priory Press, 1965.

Catechism of the Catholic Church, nos. 51–73 ("The Revelation of God"), nos. 74–100 ("The Transmission of Divine Revelation") and nos. 101–141 ("Sacred Scripture").

Green, Garrett. *Imagining God: Theology and the Religious Imagination.* San Francisco: Harper & Row, 1989.

Moran, Gabriel. *Both Sides: The Story of Revelation.* Mahwah, N.J.: Paulist, 2002.

Second Vatican Council. *Dei Verbum* (The Dogmatic Constitution on Divine Revelation), 1965.

CHAPTER SIX

Did All This Really Happen?

The Jewish New Year that began on September 25, 2004, and ended on October 3, 2005, is the year 5765. That number reflects the rabbinic calculation of the time since creation. Science has a decidedly different take on the age of the cosmos. Christian fundamentalists who, like ultra-Orthodox Jews, hold that the universe is only a few thousand years old, do admit that there does appear to be ample evidence to the contrary in fossils and geological formations and similar phenomena. They suggest, however, that God created fossils to test people's faith in the reliability of the Bible. If one can ignore the "evidence" that science adduces in support of its contention that the universe is billions of years old, then one is a true believer in the Bible as the inerrant word of God. But does faith in God and reliance on the Bible require a person to ignore well-established scientific conclusions? Was the world created in six "days" as Genesis says? Are faith and science incompatible?

Archaeology of the Bible

The book of Exodus states that the number of Hebrew slaves who left Egypt under Moses was "about six hundred thousand men on foot, besides children" (12:37). While the children were not counted, the women in the group are not even mentioned. A conservative estimate of the number of people the Bible asserts as taking part in the Exodus would be more than one million. Imagine the scope of the logistical problems associated with a journey taken by a group of this size—a journey through the wilderness of the Sinai peninsula. The Bible says that God provided the Israelites with water from a rock (Exodus 17:6) and manna (Exodus 16) as food. The State of Israel occupied the Sinai between the Six Day War of 1967 and the 1980 peace treaty with Egypt. During those thirteen years, Israeli archaeologists combed the Sinai for evidence of the Israelites' forty-year sojourn there. Excavations uncovered campfires from the Stone Age but found no evidence that there was any large-scale migration through the Sinai in the Late Bronze Age (1550–1200 B.C.) when the Israelites would have made their journey. As a result, the article on the Sinai in the *New Encyclopedia of Archaeological Excavations in the Holy Land* does not mention the Exodus. The Bible, then, remains the only testimony to this journey. One would not necessarily expect Egyptian sources to mention the departure of the Hebrew slaves, which would have been a humiliation for the Egyptians. Does this mean that the Exodus was not a historical event? Since some Christians believe that God revealed God-self in the events of ancient Israel's history, what does the absence of archaeological evidence for the Exodus say about revelation? What is the relationship between faith and history?

In 1993 and 1994 archaeologists excavating at the site of the ancient Israelite city of Dan discovered two fragments of an inscribed pillar erected by an Aramean king named Hazael in 825 B.C. to celebrate the victories of his father Hadad II over the Judahite king Jehoshaphat. One line of the inscription mentions "the house of David." This is the only reference to David in any ancient Near Eastern text outside of the Bible. Some have hailed the find as among the most significant discoveries in the Holy Land since it confirms the historical character of the Bible. A few have suggested that the inscription is a forgery. Unfortunately, there have been several such forgeries in recent years but "the house of David" inscription is still undergoing careful analysis to assess its authenticity. If the inscription is indeed authentic, it will provide important support for those who assert that the Bible can be used as a source to reconstruct the history of Israel.

Anyone who reads the Bible will have to ask and answer a basic question: "Did all this really happen?" A good portion of the Old Testament is made up of stories: the Torah (Genesis through Deuteronomy), the Former Prophets (Joshua, Judges, Samuel and Kings), the two books of Chronicles, Ezra, Nehemiah, Ruth, Esther, Judith, Tobit, 1 and 2 Maccabees. Until the nineteenth century, most readers simply assumed that these books were actual accounts of events in the life of the ancient Israelites and early Jews. Many people who read the Bible today read these stories as if they were historical accounts similar to those produced by modern historians. Because some readers consider the Bible to be the inerrant word of God, they hold that the stories of the Bible must be true accounts of actual events since God would not teach truth in a book that contained errors of any kind. Because, for example, the book of Joshua asserts that the sun and moon "stood still" (10:12–13), that settles the matter despite the obvious problem science has with such a claim. Other readers take a compromise approach by showing that miraculous events such as the plagues in Egypt (Exodus 7:14—11:10) were actually natural occurrences. What was miraculous was the timing of these events since they happened at precisely the right time, facilitating the escape of the Hebrew slaves from bondage in Egypt.

What, then, is the relationship between the stories in the Bible to the Christian faith? Are these stories simply edifying tales or are they reminiscences of actual events in Israel's history? Some biblical interpreters have claimed that the events of Israel's past are the means God chose to be revealed not only to Israel—but to the world. It follows from this claim that the events narrated in the Bible must have happened if the Bible is to have any theological value for believers today. It has become increasingly more difficult to sustain this position since the results of archaeological and historical studies have shown that the Bible cannot be used to reconstruct the events of ancient Israel's history. The stories of Israel's past as told in the Bible are the product of theological reflection and are, therefore, statements of faith rather than "histories" in the technical sense of the word. While some of the stories do have a basis in ancient Israel's historical experience, it is a mistake to ask these stories to meet the goals of the modern historian.

There is a small group of biblical interpreters who hold that the stories in the Torah and Former Prophets are propagandistic tales produced in the Hellenistic periods (fourth through second centuries B.C.) to create an identity for the Jews and to sustain their claims to political independence and economic rights. Though these views have not attracted broad support, they do suggest that careful integration of the results of archaeological work and study of ancient Near Eastern documents with biblical interpretation is necessary to make historical judgments.

The Bible on Creation

The question remains, "Did all this really happen?" We will begin formulating an answer by beginning at the beginning: the story of creation in Genesis 1:1—2:25. In the last twenty-five years, the stories of creation in Genesis have been the object of intense political struggles in several states. The first was in Arkansas, which passed a law in 1981 requiring that "creation science" be given equal time with evolution in school curricula. The courts found this law unconstitutional since "creation science" was not science and the Arkansas law to introduce it into public school curricula was a thinly veiled attempt to inject religious beliefs into these curricula. In 1987 the Supreme Court sustained this decision by asserting that laws mandating the teaching of "creation science" involved the restructuring of science curricula to accommodate a particular religious perspective. After the Supreme Court decision, some state legislatures required that a disclaimer be included in science textbooks or prefaced to any classroom discussion of the origins of the universe and life, stating that evolution is merely a theory and should not dissuade students from believing in the "biblical" teaching on creation. The courts also rejected this strategy on constitutional grounds. This led the creationists to change their strategy again. They abandoned the term "creation science" and began using the term "intelligent design" as an alternative to the teaching of evolution. The controversy continues.

Those who promote "creation science" or the "intelligent design" theory view the stories in Genesis 1—2 as the biblical account of the origin of the universe and of life on earth. They are mistaken. The majesty of the Genesis 1 account and the charm of the Genesis 2 account are certainly familiar. Genesis 1 describes the universe and all that is in it coming into existence by the simple command of God. In contrast, Genesis 2 portrays God as sculpting Adam's body from clay and then breathing life into it. But these are not the only ways that the ancient Israelites imagined creation as occurring. There are indications elsewhere in the Old Testament that they imagined the world coming into existence in a far different way than described in Genesis. Both the book of Psalms (74; 89) and the book of Job (40—41) allude to God's victory over the sea monsters Leviathan and Rahab. These monsters represented the powers of chaos that resisted God's creative activity.

Israel's vision of creation as the result of God's momentous struggle with chaotic powers residing in the sea shows similarity to patterns of expression common in the ancient Near

East. The ancients viewed the sea as a cosmic element whose power had to be held in check so that an ordered world could emerge. The Babylonian account of creation, which Genesis 1 adapted in part, tells of Marduk (Babylon's patron deity) killing Tiamat (the sea), and forming the heavens and earth from its corpse. The author of Genesis 1 omits the story of the conflict with the sea except for the enigmatic phrase at the very beginning of the story: "…darkness covered the face of the deep while a wind from God swept over the face of the waters" (verse 2b) and the description of what existed before God's creative word as "a formless void" (verse 2a). The Genesis 1 adaptation of the Babylonian story suppresses details of any struggle with the forces of chaos, but has God's words speaking the universe into existence. The idea of creation by a divine word, however, did not originate with the ancient Israelites. The Egyptians, whose religious imagination devised several creation accounts, developed one that portrayed the god Ptah as creating the world by simply speaking it into existence.

The people of the ancient Near East were as fascinated by their world as we are by ours. In attempting to understand the world's mysteries, they gave full play to their imagination. The result was a number of stories about the origins of the cosmos. While these stories may differ in details, they all agree that the world was the creation of divine power that brought order out of chaos and that only divine power kept the world from reverting to chaos. One way that people today express their fascination with our world is through the lens of scientific discovery. These two ways of approaching the world and its mysteries are not contradictory but simply different. Science cannot move beyond the study of observable phenomena from the tiniest organism visible only through a microscope to immense galaxies accessible only through gigantic telescopes. Faith moves beyond phenomena, seeing beyond what is visible. Here is the point at which believers today find the language created by ancient believers both helping and hindering at the same time. Speaking of the world's creation in biblical categories puts believers at a distance from those who limit their encounter with creation to the phenomenal level. Using biblical language to express their wonder at the world and all that is in it allows believers to move from the observation of creation to belief in the Creator.

To transform the stories of Genesis into bearers of scientific or historical fact is to misuse them. These stories are the product of religious imagination celebrating the world and human life as gifts from God. The diverse ways that the peoples of the ancient Near East—the ancient Israelites included—spoke of creation is a testimony to both their literary creativity and their religious faith. Some contemporary readers of these stories are asking for something Genesis cannot give: a scientific explanation for the origins of the universe and human life. "Creation science" cannot achieve the goals it sets out for itself because it requires support from first millennium B.C. religious texts to overturn hypotheses that all reputable scientists use as the basis for their attempts to understand the physical world. That the world was created and is sustained by God is an affirmation that is beyond the potential of science to affirm or deny. Prompted by a faith-filled reading of the Genesis stories, the believer can do nothing more than join the psalmist in praise of the Creator:

> O LORD, our Sovereign,
>> how majestic is your name in all the earth!

> You have set your glory above the heavens.
>> Out of the mouths of babes and infants
> you have founded a bulwark because of your foes,
>> to silence the enemy and the avenger.

> When I look at your heavens, the work of your fingers,
>> the moon and the stars that you have established;
> what are human beings that you are mindful of them,
>> mortals that you care for them?

> Yet you have made them a little lower than God,
>> and crowned them with glory and honor.
> You have given them dominion over the works of your
>> hands;
>> you have put all things under their feet,
> all sheep and oxen,
>> and also the beasts of the field,
> the birds of the air, and the fish of the sea,
>> whatever passes along the paths of the seas.

> O LORD, our Sovereign,
>> how majestic is your name in all the earth!
> (Psalm 8)

Israel Acquires the Land of Canaan

While many people have no problem recognizing that the stories in the first chapters of Genesis are faith-inspired tales rather than sources of scientific data, they often have a problem recognizing the character of stories about Israel's life in its land. They read like eyewitness accounts of actual events. But a careful reader of the biblical "histories" notices that there are problems in reading them as straightforward historical accounts. For example, consider the stories of how Israel acquired the territory that was the scene of its subsequent history: the land of Israel. That story occupies two books: Joshua and Judges. Even a superficial reading of these two books reveals serious problems if one wishes to use these books as sources to reconstruct the events that led to ancient Israel's acquisition of Canaan as its homeland.

According to the book of Joshua, the Israelites acquired Canaan by means of military conquest. The book describes the conquest of the land and the distribution of the conquered territories among the Israelite tribes. In telling its story, the book of Joshua follows a geographical arrangement that makes good sense. The book begins with God ordering Joshua to lead the Israelite tribes westward across the River Jordan into the center of Canaan. The story of the river crossing and associated events take up chapters 2 through 5. The actual conquest takes place by the militia of the Israelite tribes united under Joshua's leadership. A military campaign begins in the center of Canaan (chapters 6 through 8) and is followed by another directed to the south (chapters 9 through 10) and a third to the north (chapter 11). Chapter 12 lists the territories taken and the Canaanite kings defeated. The division of the conquered territories among the victorious Israelites takes up chapters 13 through 21. The results of these wars of conquest are summarized in Joshua 11:23:

So Joshua took the whole land, according to all that the
LORD had spoken to Moses; and Joshua gave it for an
inheritance to Israel according to their tribal allotments.
And the land had rest from war.

The book concludes with Joshua's farewell to the Israelites,
the renewal of the covenant and a notice of Joshua's death
and burial (Joshua 23—24).

When one turns the page to the book of Judges, it is as if the
Israelite victories under Joshua never happened. Judges
begins with a question posed by the Israelites to God following the death of Joshua: "Who shall go up first for us against
the Canaanites, to fight against them?" (Judges 1:1b).

Instead of controlling the whole of Canaan, the book of
Judges portrays the Israelites as living in enclaves scattered
about the region and constantly threatened by more powerful neighbors. Also, Judges tells of a downward spiral of
Israel's fortunes due to its moral deterioration. Though God
raises up several "judges" to halt this downward spiral, it
appears that matters get progressively worse until Israel is on
the brink of self-destruction. Also in Judges, the tribes do not
act in concert as they did in Joshua, but in small groupings;
neither do they enjoy a string of military successes as they
did under his leadership. Their hold on the land is piece-
meal and tenuous. The books of Joshua and Judges tell two
different stories about how Israelites acquired their land,
and historians had to find a way to deal with these differences as they attempted to reconstruct the events that led to
Israel's control of the land of Canaan.

One approach was to simply choose one book over the other as a source to reconstruct ancient Israel's early history. Those historians who chose the book of Joshua as their source hold that Israel's control of Canaan came by way of military conquest. The book of Judges reflects a later time when Israel's infidelity brought divine judgment in the form of military defeat at the hands of the Canaanites. The discrepancies between Joshua and Judges could be explained if we simply had more information. Lacking that, readers ought to take the stories of Joshua and Judges at face value. Those historians who held that the book of Judges more accurately described the land-taking suggested that Israel acquired its land by a gradual process of infiltration rather than an invasion of tribal armies. For the most part, this infiltration was a peaceful process though occasionally the interests of the Israelites and the Canaanites clashed, leading to local conflicts similar to the ones described in Judges.

If ancient Israel's literature could not provide an unambiguous answer to the problems of reconstructing history, perhaps its material remains could. Historians and biblical interpreters turned to archaeology for help. Unfortunately, the results of excavations complicated the situation. For example, excavators at Jericho found only meager material remains from the Late Bronze Age (1550–1200 B.C.) when the Israelite tribes were thought to have made their appearance in Canaan. Though the Bible describes a miraculous destruction of Jericho's walls (see Joshua 6), there is no archaeological evidence that Jericho was a walled town at the time the ancient Israelites supposedly conquered it. Following the Israelite victory at Jericho, the book of Joshua says that the tribal army moved on to Ai. Archaeological work there revealed that Ai was an Early Bronze Age (3300–1950 B.C.) city that was destroyed and rebuilt several times. A final and decisive destruction took place in 2550 B.C.—more than a thousand years before the Israelite tribes could have destroyed it. These excavations, however, do help explain the improbable name the Bible gives to the city. The Hebrew word Ai means "ruin." Clearly evidence of the city's destruction was visible for anyone to see, and the author of Joshua simply assumed that the Israelite militia under Joshua was responsible for it.

Excavations at Hazor, however, do show violent destruction at the time the Israelite settlement took place. It is tempting to identify that destruction with the story in Joshua 11:10–15, which tells of the conquest of Hazor by the Israelite tribes under Joshua. But excavations have not been able to identify those responsible. The end of the Late Bronze Age was a time of considerable social and political dislocation and strife throughout the eastern Mediterranean region; it is just not possible to say definitively that the Israelites were responsible for the fall of Hazor.

It is clear, however, from full-scale excavations and surveys of the central highlands of Israel that there is no archaeological evidence to support the accounts of a military conquest of the area by Joshua and the Israelite tribes. These investigations make it clear that there was no large-scale invasion from the east. Instead, it seems more likely that the Israelite tribes were formed, in large part, from the people who fled to the safety of the hills to avoid the incessant and debilitating wars between the Canaanite city-states. Two important technological developments made agricultural settlements possible in those hills: The invention of the iron-tipped plow made it possible to work the rocky soil of the highlands, and the development of the cistern enabled farmers to store an adequate supply of water to get them through the dry season.

According to this scenario, religious undergirding for this withdrawal from obligations to the oppressive Canaanite regimes was provided by the ideology of a small group of Hebrew slaves who escaped from Egypt. These escaped slaves spoke of a God who took the side of the poor and oppressed against their overlords. The other peasants of the Canaanite hill country made the ideology of the Hebrews their own. The Canaanite villagers identified with the escaped slaves and, in time, adopted the story of the Exodus and Sinai as their own. From these people eventually developed the two Israelite national states: Israel in the north and Judah in the south. Both worshiped Yahweh and derived their identity from the story of the Exodus and Sinai experiences.

If the stories in Joshua and Judges cannot be used to reconstruct the history of the Israelite settlement in Canaan, what is their function in the Bible? It is important to remember that the division of the Bible into separate books is sometimes artificial. This is particularly true about the books of Joshua, Judges, Samuel and Kings. Originally, these books comprised the story of Israel in its land from the settlement of the tribes in Canaan to the exile of the people of Judah to Babylon. These "books" were simply part of a single story believed to have been composed, in its present form, by a single person. Any attempt at appreciating the contribution of Joshua and Judges in the biblical tradition must begin with the recognition that the stories in these books are part of a much larger work. The rabbis named this larger work the "Former Prophets," because they believed that the story of Israel in its land was written under prophetic inspiration—principally by Samuel and Jeremiah. Modern students of the Bible call this larger work the "Deuteronomistic history" since the theological perspectives that are interwoven in the story of Israel in its land derive from the book of Deuteronomy. Simply stated, Deuteronomy holds that blessings come into Israel's life as a consequence of its commitment to the Torah; failure to live in obedience to the Torah brings disaster.

Despite the name scholars generally use for it, the Deuteronomistic history is not a history in the technical sense of the word. It was not written by eyewitnesses of the events it depicts, nor was it based on eyewitness accounts— for the most part. It is more in the nature of a homiletic reflection on Israel's experience in its land from the time of the settlement to the time of the exile. One purpose of this reflection is to explain what happened—why what began with so much promise ended in tragedy. But a more significant goal was providing the exile with hope for the future. In a sense, then, the Deuteronomistic history turns the past into a sermon that aims to motivate the exiles to obey the written law of the book of Deuteronomy. That book makes it clear that Israel has only two alternatives: obedience and life or disobedience and death (see Deuteronomy 30:15–20). The books of Joshua and Judges are example stories of what happens when Israel makes its choice. According to Joshua 24:31, "Israel served the LORD all the days of Joshua." It is little wonder then that the Israelites "took the whole land" and enjoyed the blessing of peace and prosperity in that land (see Joshua 11:23). The book of Judges asserts that after Joshua's death, "...the Israelites did what was evil in the sight of the LORD and worshiped the Baals; and they abandoned the LORD...who had brought them out of the land of Egypt..." (Judges 2:11–12). The book then describes the downward spiral of disobedience and judgment that brought Israel to the brink of self-destruction.

The books of Joshua and Judges are theological works that present their religious teachings through storytelling. Modern readers are not accustomed to stories as a medium of theological or religious discourse. But to treat these books as if they were historical documents is to misread them. This is not to say that these books contain no historical information. But distilling that information from these theological reflections is not a simple matter. Again, readers should not ask a text to do something that it cannot do; rather, they should accept the text on its own terms so that there can be genuine and fruitful dialogue between text and reader. Reading Joshua and Judges as religious texts with important theological content will allow the texts to be themselves.

Listening to the Text
Allowing the text to be itself—this is the key to any fruitful encounter with the Bible. The reader needs to listen to the text. But this listening, to be authentic, must be open to the text's cultural and religious perspectives. Once this careful

and informed listening takes place, believers can use their experience, imagination and creativity to have the biblical text inform and shape their conversion, their life of faith. If readers look to the Bible for scientific and historical information, they miss the real contribution Old Testament narratives can make to the Christian life. For believers, the biblical stories are not about what happened at the beginning of time or about what happened to another people at another time. They are about what God is doing in the present. God's creative activity is still going on, but to discern that activity requires the faith of a person willing to see beyond phenomena. The stories of Genesis help the believer to see God's presence and power in creation—a presence and power obscured by human selfishness and sin that blinds our eyes and dulls our comprehension. The God who created the universe calls us to choose life, and the Old Testament stories provide example after example of the consequences of the choices that we make. These stories serve to move us to faith and obedience—if we allow them to be themselves.

A problem that some Christians have in reading Old Testament stories as bearers of religious truth is what they regard as a denial of the miraculous by the rationalism of the modern era. Because we do not think "miracles" happen, they do not happen. There are events that defy explanation in the lives of individuals and of nations. When such events happen, we thank God for them, but we are always ready to accept a scientific explanation. Such an explanation ought not diminish a believer's gratitude. The "miraculous" are elements in biblical stories by which the storyteller underscores God's presence in Israel's life and God's activity on Israel's behalf. The story of a miracle, then, is not so much a report of what happened as much as it is an affirmation of faith and gratitude—which call for a response of loving obedience from the believer. Still, there are some believers who maintain that, since Jesus taught some of these legendary events as history, that must be the case. For example, Jesus said that "Jonah was three days and three nights in the belly of the sea monster" (Matthew 12:41). Jesus, as the Son of God, could not teach something erroneous, and until the modern era, the historicity of the book of Jonah was simply taken for granted—as was the historicity of the Bible as a whole. We must remember, though, that Jesus was speaking to people who took the book of Jonah at face value, and he used this to teach about the importance of repentance (see Matthew 12:38–41). We do not need to assert the historical accuracy of the Jonah story to sustain Jesus' teaching, as is evident in the Lucan version of this incident, which does not mention Jonah in the belly of the great fish (see Luke 11:29–32). In addition, Jesus can and did teach by using stories. Indeed, a favorite form of his teaching was through parables—fictional tales.

"Did all this really happen?" That may be the wrong question to ask. Old Testament stories turn the past into a sermon. Their goal is not to provide historical, verifiable information about the past, but to motivate people to fidelity in the present. In other words, these stories are not about "them"; they are about us and our life with God. Unless we read them as about the present, we strip them of their power to shape our lives as believers. We cannot afford to let this happen. When we read the stories of the escaped Hebrew slaves, the

Israelite militia, oppressed Israelite farmers, the prophet Jonah in the belly of the great fish, we are reading stories about ourselves. These stories are mirrors in which we see reflected our own life with God. That is their real power— the stories of the Old Testament help us see how we are and who God is.

QUESTIONS FOR REFLECTION

1. How does the historical truth of Old Testament stories relate to their religious value?

2. How did ancient Israel acquire the land that was the scene of its subsequent history?

3. What are the several ways that the Bible affirms the ancient Israelite belief that Israel's God was responsible for the creation of the universe?

4. Evaluate this statement: "The events narrated in the Bible had to have happened."

5. What is the value of Old Testament stories for the Christian believer today?

FOR FURTHER READING

Alter, Robert. *The Art of Biblical Narrative*. New York: Basic Books, 1981.

McCurley, Foster R. *Ancient Myths and Biblical Faith: Scriptural Transformations*. Philadelphia: Fortress, 1983.

McDermott, John J. *What Are They Saying about the Formation of Israel?* Mahwah, N.J.: Paulist, 1998.

Smith, Mark S. *The Memoirs of God: History, Memory, and the Experience of the Divine in Ancient Israel*. Minneapolis: Augsburg Fortress, 2004.

CHAPTER SEVEN

How Do We Find Meaning
in the Old Testament?

T hose who sit on the United States Supreme Court try to determine what light the U.S. Constitution sheds on the disputes brought before it. The justices rarely render unanimous decisions because they do not all read the Constitution in the same way. The decisions they render are not always met with acceptance because individuals and groups of Americans also read the Constitution differently. Consider the reaction in the South to the 1954 Supreme Court decision which held that segregation in public schools was unconstitutional, or the continuing controversy around the 1973 Supreme Court decision that created a legal right to abortion. Unanswered questions abound: The Civil War was fought, in part, over whether states had the constitutional right to secede from the Union. Is there a right to privacy since such a right is not mentioned in the Constitution? Does the First Amendment forbidding the establishment of any religion by the government mean that prayers may not be offered in public schools? Does the Second Amendment make any gun control laws unconstitutional?

The Constitution of the United States is a relatively short document, fairly recently written (little more than two hundred years old) and written in English, the mother tongue of the vast majority of Americans. Yet, there are serious disagreements as to what the document says and what it implies.

If it is difficult to read and interpret the Constitution, how much more challenging must it be to read and interpret the Old Testament? This collection of books comes from a culture quite different from that of twenty-first century America. It is written in languages (Hebrew, Aramaic and Greek) which very few Americans can read. It reflects experiences that many contemporary readers do not have. How can readers today derive significant meaning from texts that, on the surface, appear so alien to contemporary thought, culture and experience? Is the Old Testament little more than a relic from our collective religious past with very little significance for believers today? To believe in the Bible, do we have to forget what we know from science, reason and experience? Does taking the Old Testament seriously mean we have to think literally and live like the ancient nomads?

Reading Different Kinds of Texts

The meaning of any text—as simple as a friendly letter or as complex as the Constitution—is not immediately self-evident. It takes some skill to read different kinds of texts. We learn how to read letters from an aunt who always thinks in worst-case scenarios and from a cousin who is a bit of a Pollyanna.

We can discriminate news reports we read in the *New York Times* from those in the *National Enquirer*. We know the difference between a novel about the Battle of Gettysburg like Michael Shaara's *The Killer Angels* and a historical treatment like Stephen Sears's *Gettysburg*. We are aware that although Karl Rahner's *Theological Investigations* and the *Catechism of the Catholic Church* may touch on the same subjects, their treatment of these subjects will be dissimilar.

Good study Bibles such as the *Catholic Study Bible* or *The New Oxford Annotated Bible* help readers appreciate the differences between the various types of literature that are found in the Bible: stories, hymns, laws, genealogies, proverbs, prophecies. Commentaries provide a model of how to approach these different kinds of texts—how to read them with a measure of understanding, sympathy and appreciation. Still, there is a common misconception about biblical literature that can prevent readers from experiencing the full power of Old Testament texts. Some readers imagine the process of interpretation to be similar to distillation. Awareness of the historical, literary and cultural dimensions of the text enables us to "distill" these out until we have the "pure" religious meaning of these texts freed from the complicating and unfamiliar cultural and literary forms that can obscure that meaning. The pure religious meaning of the text is universally valid, transcending culture and time. The goal of biblical study and interpretation, then, is to find this theological core of individual biblical texts—this universally valid meaning that is "hidden" in the text. There is one feature of texts, however, that suggests that the goal of finding the meaning of biblical texts is misguided.

Finding meaning in any text is the result of the interplay between text and reader. The reader is not simply a passive recipient of information, but someone actively investing the text with meaning. Reading the Bible is really a conversation between our ancestors in the faith and us. It is faith speaking to faith.

The books of the Old Testament come from different kinds of people: prophets, sages, elders, poets, priests, teachers. Not all these people lived at the same time, nor did they have the same kind of experience. We should expect to notice differences in how they speak of ancient Israel's encounter with its God. Similarly, there are all sorts of differences among the people who read these ancient texts, looking for light and life. The most significant of these differences goes under the general heading of social location.

The Role of the Reader

The social location of a reader refers to characteristics such as age, gender, nationality, race, health, career, social class, personality type and marital status—things that make one reader different from another. Readers who share certain aspects of social location tend to understand texts in similar ways; those with a different social location are likely to understand the words differently.

For example, until about fifty years ago, most biblical interpreters were teachers in seminaries, schools of theology or denominational colleges and universities. It was their responsibility to prepare pastors, priests, teachers and church workers. Most of these teachers in these settings were white, male, European or American, and were usually ordained priests or ministers themselves. The questions they asked of the text were remarkably similar. Though they may have derived different answers, they used the same methods of biblical interpretation—they spoke the same "language."

More recently in the United States, there has been a significant shift in the academic setting of professional biblical studies. While seminaries and schools of theology are still important centers for biblical research and teaching, the Bible has become the object of study in public, nonsectarian and private colleges and universities. In these settings, the kinds of questions asked of the biblical text and the types of methods used to elicit answers are quite different. In the setting of a secular university, the focus might be on the Bible as literature, or on the history of ancient Israelite and early Jewish religion.

Different questions have led to different answers by way of different analytical methods. All of this has enriched the process of biblical interpretation. But nowhere has the shift in the social location of biblical interpreters been more obvious and influential than in the growth of the numbers of female biblical scholars. This development can be explained, in part, by the relatively recent practice, in most Christian churches, of ordaining women. But in the United States, the more important influence in the development of biblical studies from a woman's perspective has been the women's movement. This movement has led women to make career choices beyond "traditional" female roles. These new sets of eyes reading the biblical text has enriched biblical studies—something the Pontifical Biblical Commission noted in its 1993 document, *The Interpretation of the Bible in the Church:*

Women have played a more active part in exegetical research. They have succeeded, often better than men, in detecting the presence, the significance and the role of women in the Bible, in Christian origins and in the church. The worldview of today, because of its greater attention to the dignity of women and to their role in society and in the church, ensures that new questions are put to the biblical text, which in turn occasions new discoveries. Feminine sensitivity helps to unmask and correct certain commonly accepted interpretations which were tendentious and sought to justify the male domination of women. (I.E.2)

Also, there has been an increasing number of biblical scholars coming from outside Europe and North America. There have been several publishing projects, such as the International Theological Commentary series (Eerdmans), that have sought to make the work of these scholars available to a wider audience. These scholars from Africa, Asia and Central and South America have put new questions to the text, which has enriched the process of finding meaning.

Identifying With Characters
Related to the enriching of biblical scholarship with the rise of women and international biblical scholars is the issue of empathy in reading biblical stories. Very often, readers' social locations will determine the characters with whom they identify. In fact, what makes Bible stories so attractive are their "true to life" characters. People want to read these stories because of the characters for whom they can feel some empathy.

For example, Genesis 16 and 21 tell the story of tensions within Abraham's family. Unable to conceive, his wife Sarah offered Abraham her Egyptian servant Hagar as a secondary wife. But as soon as Hagar became pregnant, she reveled in her new higher standing within Abraham's family, leading Sarah to have Abraham expel Hagar. An "angel" (a circumlocution for God) advised Hagar to return and reassume her status as Sarah's servant. Genesis 21 relates a similar story. It notes that shortly after Isaac was weaned, Sarah had Abraham send Hagar and her child Ishmael away. Again, an "angel" appeared, assuring Hagar that God heard her child's cries and that God had a great future in store for Ishmael. Women reading this story might focus on the tension between Sarah and Hagar and find that this tension is caused by a social system in which women, to have any value, need to produce male offspring. This system pitted Sarah against Hagar as they vied for the limited resources of Abraham's household. Abraham did nothing to effect reconciliation between the two but allowed the conflict to take its course.

The problem, then, is not between Sarah and Hagar; it is with Abraham and the system of patriarchy that he supports. Hagar could represent all exploited, abused and rejected women. She might gain the sympathy of a woman who faces her pregnancy alone, a wife who is divorced for the sake of another woman, a mother on public assistance, a homeless woman, the woman who serves others only to find herself abandoned. Similarly, poor people who read this story might identify with Hagar and Ishmael. They are the voiceless and nameless poor. Neither Hagar nor Ishmael speaks in these stories, and Ishmael is not even mentioned by name in Genesis 21. But in the end, God ensures that Ishmael is blessed abundantly since injustice—no matter who the perpetrator and no matter who the victim—is not ignored by God. The older approach taken to these narratives tended to focus on Abraham and his need to have an heir so that the promise made to him by God might be fulfilled, but new eyes have reread this story, leading to new insight and new meaning.

Similarly, imagine with whom Palestinian Christians identify as they read the stories of Joshua and Judges that describe how Israel acquired the land. Clearly, these stories raise theological problems for them as they reflect on their own experience of being dispossessed of the land that had been their home for hundreds of years. What does God's election of Jacob and his family mean for the Canaanites who live in the land? Why must they be expelled to provide a home for the escaped Hebrew slaves? Where are the Canaanites to go? How can the violent conflicts over the land be justified? Where is the divine justice in the expulsion and annihilation of the indigenous peoples of Canaan? Palestinian Christians reading the biblical stories of ancient Israel's conquest of Canaan find the events described in these stories recurring in their own experience of expulsion and occupation. Rather than finding "light and life" in these biblical narratives, such readers are troubled and confused. How could they sing the praises of a God who allows such things to happen?

The book of Job is one of those biblical texts that cannot be read just once. Reading Job in the midst of personal tragedy is quite different from reading it in times of tranquility. The book takes on a whole new meaning for the reader who is experiencing something of what Job experienced. The prayer "...the LORD gave, and the LORD has taken away; blessed be the name of the LORD" (Job 1:21b) is more than a pious sentiment when read by someone who has to deal with loss and grief. Similarly, the reader who is dealing with frustrations that seem to have no end—when nothing seems to make sense—finds a kindred spirit in Ecclesiastes who describes how he felt under similar experiences when he wrote, "It is all vanity and a chasing after wind" (Ecclesiastes 4:4). Social location and empathy—these are decisive in the search for meaning.

Reading Strategy

In addition to social location and empathy, a third significant influence on a text's meaning is reading strategy. The way a reader encounters a text helps shape the way that text is understood. Many Catholics encounter texts from the Old Testament as lessons read during worship. On most Sundays and holy days, the first lesson is taken from the Old Testament. The weekday lectionary also contains Old Testament lessons. These lessons are short excerpts from much longer works. Reading these lessons as "freestanding" works is quite different from reading a text as components of much larger works. Also, the Old Testament lessons for the Sunday liturgy are usually chosen to illuminate the Gospel lesson, so one almost never encounters the Old Testament lessons on their own terms.

For example, the first reading for the twenty-eighth Sunday of Ordinary Time (cycle C) is an excerpt from the story of

Elisha's healing of Naaman from leprosy (2 Kings 5:14–17). The Gospel lesson is Jesus' healing of the ten lepers on his way to Jerusalem (Luke 17:11–19). The parallels between the two readings are obvious. Naaman is a Syrian who comes to Israel for healing; of the lepers, only a foreigner (a Samaritan) returns to thank Jesus for his healing. The differences are also significant: Elisha requires Naaman to wash seven times in the Jordan River to effect his healing while Jesus cures the ten lepers by his word alone. In its setting in the lectionary, the story of Naaman's healing is merely an introduction to the more significant healing that Jesus performs. But reading the story of Naaman's healing as part of the Elisha cycle (2 Kings 2—9), which, in turn, is part of the books of Kings, which, in turn, is part of the Former Prophets (Joshua to 2 Kings), allows the reader to see that story in quite a different light. Encountering the Old Testament solely as lessons in the liturgy is like reading portions of a novel at random without ever reading the novel from beginning to end. Certainly, the meaning derived from these two reading strategies can be very dissimilar.

Another reading strategy is related to the origin of these texts as oral literature. The prophets were preachers; they proclaimed their oracles aloud. Reading these aloud can give the reader a sense of immediacy—the feeling of being personally addressed. The psalms were the hymnbook of the Jerusalem temple. These compositions were meant to be sung in a liturgical setting. Singing the psalms—or at least hearing them sung—likewise allows believers today to feel what the psalmists were trying to convey in their compositions. Even hearing biblical narratives read aloud by a skilled and sensitive reader can be a means to greater understanding. The "traditional" translation of Psalm 1:2 ("…and on his law they meditate day and night") derives from the ancient Greek and Latin translations of this psalm. The Hebrew verb, however, refers to the sounds people make as they read and reread the Torah aloud. Meditation refers to a quiet, internal reflection on the text, but the Hebrew text of Psalm 1 assumes that people read the Torah aloud. Reading the Bible aloud can lead the way to another dimension of understanding.

The Meaning of Meaning
Perhaps the most significant determinative of meaning is the reader's conception of what constitutes the "meaning" of a text. There are at least two ways to understand meaning. The more common of the two sees the meaning of a text in the cognitive message to be passed from author to reader. Until recently, the methodology of biblical interpretation focused on trying to determine that message as objectively as possible, because the content of revelation was seen to have resided in that message. Biblical interpreters developed a variety of methods to bridge the cultural and temporal gap separating author and reader so that the latter would not impose contemporary perspectives on an ancient text and thereby read meanings "into the text" rather than discovering meaning already "in the text."

Another approach to meaning identifies meaning with the affective or emotive response produced in the reader through the experience of receiving the text. Certainly the biblical text is quite different from a grocery list, a utility bill or a mass mailing. The text is designed to evoke a response from the reader. An effective text is one that does just that. Texts guide, constrain and control reading by the use of linguistic, stylistic and literary techniques. There are always "gaps" in the text that allow and, indeed, invite readers to bring their own experiences and preoccupations to the text. A person with a chronic illness may read and experience biblical stories of miraculous healings differently than will a healthy person. The slaves in the pre–Civil War South heard the story of the Exodus as a harbinger of their liberation, while their masters saw in it the incitement to "servile insurrection." People who live on the margins of society respond more enthusiastically to apocalyptic texts than do people from the upper and middle classes.

Sometimes these reactions are dismissed as "subjective" and are considered less reliable than an "objective" reading of a text. But there is no purely objective reading—especially of a text such as the Bible. The goal of the biblical writers was less to inform their readers than it was to move them—move them to faith and obedience. To achieve this purpose it is essential that the text engage the reader, touch the reader, move the reader. Biblical literature is revelatory only when it is read. Reading the text, then, is an event—something that happens when a reader interacts with the biblical text.

Reading and understanding the Bible should not be as complicated a problem as resolving difficult questions of constitutional law. Still, the meaning and significance of the Bible are not immediately self-evident. A classic literary text such as the Old Testament, which has been read continuously for three thousand years, engages readers on several levels, opening up different avenues of meaning across time and culture. The social location of readers, their reading strategy, their empathy choice, and their understanding of what "meaning" is all contribute to their understanding and appreciation of the biblical text, which can open up for sensitive and careful readers a kaleidoscope of meaning. Far from obscuring the revelatory nature of Scripture, such a kaleidoscope of meaning makes it possible for the Bible to fulfill its purpose, which is to lead every reader to greater faith and commitment.

QUESTIONS FOR REFLECTION

1. Describe your social location. How does it affect your reading of the Old Testament?
2. With which biblical characters do you most easily identify? Why?
3. Can you describe an instance of how reading the Bible aloud affected you profoundly?
4. What is the goal of revelation as found in the Bible, and how does the Old Testament meet that goal?
5. Why do you think that believers continue to find "light and life" in the Old Testament?

FOR FURTHER READING

Bird, Phyllis A. *Missing Persons and Mistaken Identities: Women and Gender in Ancient Israel.* Philadelphia: Fortress, 1997.

Boff, Clodovis, and Jorge V. Pixley. *The Bible, the Church, and the Poor.* Maryknoll, N.Y.: Orbis, 1989.

Felder, Cain Hope, ed., *Stony the Road We Trod: African American Biblical Interpretation.* Philadelphia: Fortress, 1991.

McKenzie, Stephen L. and Stephen R. Hayes. *To Each Its Own Meaning: An Introduction to Biblical Criticisms and Their Application.* Louisville: Westminster John Knox, 1993.

Pontifical Biblical Commission. *The Interpretation of the Bible in the Church.* Boston: Daughters of St. Paul, 1993.

Sugirtharajah, Rasiah. S., ed. *Voices From the Margin: Interpreting the Bible in the Third World,* second ed. Maryknoll, N.Y.: Orbis, 1995.

Suleiman, Susan, and Inge Crosman. *The Reader in the Text: Essays on Audience and Interpretation.* Princeton, N.J.: Princeton University Press, 1980.

CONCLUSION

Finding meaning in the Old Testament is not an elusive goal. While these Scriptures come from another culture, another age, another religion, they can engage Christians today—if they bring their experience, their hopes, their questions, their doubts and their faith into conversation with the text. They will find that the Old Testament is not as alien as they imagined. The people who first heard and read these texts were believers themselves who were trying to come to grips with their own religious beliefs and commitments—trying to comprehend the dimensions and consequences of their encounter with the Divine. There is an authentic commonality between the people to whom the prophets first spoke and those who hear the prophets speak again today.

This is not to say that there are no obstacles that stand in the way of those who look for meaning in the Scriptures today. Communicating across cultural boundaries is never a simple matter, and those who read the Old Testament need to cross formidable temporal boundaries as well. But the Bible continues to be the object of intensive study whose goal is to facilitate the conversation between the people who produced and transmitted the biblical texts and the people who read them today. This study has produced widely available scholarly and popular resources that illuminate the path of anyone wishing to read the Bible with a measure of understanding. This book has attempted to show that the distance separating us from the people of ancient Israel and early Judaism is not as great as it may appear. They believed in a God who loved and cared for them. They believed that they were called by God to be instruments of blessing in the world. They believed in a God who revealed the divine will to them and who called them to obedience. We believe the very same things about ourselves.

The Old Testament need not be strange territory for readers today—any more than are Homer's *Iliad* or Shakespeare's *Hamlet*. Reading the Old Testament is a lot like reading any example of classic literature. It takes some doing at times, but the rewards are great. Classic literature is classic because it speaks to generation after generation of readers, never losing its ability to entertain, to enthrall, to enliven. All classic literature has an indefinable—almost indescribable—power that sets it apart from even other literary works. For people of faith the Old Testament has a power that sets it apart from other classic texts: the power of God who reaches from the heavens to touch the lives of God's human creatures. Speaking in the name of God, the prophet tells of this power:

> For as the rain and the snow come down from heaven
>   and do not return there until they have watered the
>   earth,

making it bring forth and sprout
  giving seed to the sower and bread to the eater,
so shall my word be that goes out from my mouth;
  it shall not return to me empty,
but it shall accomplish that which I purpose,
  and succeed in the thing for which I sent it.
(Isaiah 55:10–11)

INDEX